Editorial Project Manager
Erica N. Russikoff, M.A.

Editor in Chief
Karen J. Goldfluss, M.S. Ed.

Creative Director
Sarah M. Fournier

Illustrator
Mark Mason

Art Coordinator
Renée Mc Elwee

Cover Artist
Diem Pascarella

Imaging
Amanda R. Harter

Publisher
Mary D. Smith, M.S. Ed.

Author
Tracie Heskett, M. Ed.

For correlations to the Common Core State Standards, see pages 107–112 of this book or visit *http://www.teachercreated.com/standards/*.

Teacher Created Resources
12621 Western Avenue
Garden Grove, CA 92841
www.teachercreated.com
ISBN: 978-1-4206-8388-2

Made in U.S.A.

Table of Contents

Introduction

Approaching Math Content—Today's Standards

The Common Core State Standards address several important goals in education:

- to prepare students for college and careers
- to develop critical-thinking and analytical skills students need for success
- to help teachers measure student progress and achievement throughout the year

The Common Core Mathematics Standards seek to provide teachers and students with focused mathematics instruction. The standards are designed to deepen students' understanding as they progress through grade levels and topics.

Mathematics is a subject in which concepts build in a progression. A strong foundation of basic concepts must be laid, beginning in the early grades. The Common Core State Standards recognize this learning sequence. Mathematical thinking is divided into several broad categories, referred to as "domains." Elementary grades address the same general domains, with specific standards for student understanding and achievement within each domain. For grades 1–5, these domains include Operations & Algebraic Thinking, Number & Operations in Base Ten, Number & Operations—Fractions (begins in grade 3), Measurement & Data, and Geometry.

It is important for students to understand the role mathematics plays in everyday life. The Common Core Mathematics Standards encourage students to apply their mathematical knowledge to real-world problems and situations. Teachers, in turn, assess student understanding and mastery of concepts by asking them to explain their thinking and justify their answers. Word problems provide students with opportunities for the practical application of mathematical concepts.

This book presents word problems in a realistic setting. Students dig into the content of each "scenario" as they apply math concepts to solve multiple problems. Each unit is designed to encourage students to read for understanding, revisit content on a variety of levels, and use information as a tool for solving more complex problems.

Establishing Mathematical Practices

The Common Core Standards for Mathematical Practice (SMP) describe practices students can implement to help them engage with mathematical content. As your students work through the activities in this book, encourage them to develop these habits as they practice and develop problem-solving skills.

1. Make sense of problems and persevere in solving them.
2. Reason abstractly and quantitatively.
3. Construct viable arguments and critique the reasoning of others.
4. Model with mathematics.
5. Use appropriate tools strategically.
6. Attend to precision.
7. Look for and make use of structure.
8. Look for and express regularity in repeated reasoning.

These practices help students understand core mathematical concepts so they can apply a variety of strategies for successful problem solving. As students learn underlying principles, they will be able to . . .

- consider similar problems.
- represent problems in ways that make sense.
- justify conclusions and explain their reasoning.
- apply mathematics to practical situations.
- use technology to work with mathematics.
- explain concepts to other students.
- consider a broad overview of a problem.
- deviate from a known procedure to use an appropriate shortcut.
- reason and explain why a mathematical statement is true.
- explain and apply appropriate mathematical rules.

Help your students and their families find success. Work with administrators, other teachers, and parents to plan and hold math-coaching nights for parents. The tips on page 6 may be helpful for parents as they work with students at home. Consider photocopying the page to send home in students' homework folders to aid with math assignments. Additionally, prepare a visual aid to help parents understand students' work in math. Share this aid with parents at back-to-school night or on other occasions when they visit the classroom.

How to Use This Book

This book contains several mathematical problem-solving units. Each unit gives students the opportunity to practice and develop one or more essential mathematical skills. Units are grouped by domains—although within a unit, more than one domain may be addressed. Within each domain, math concepts build on one another, forming a foundation for student learning and understanding. In addition to the Common Core Mathematics Standards covered in this book, the passages that accompany each unit meet one or more English Language Arts Standards as they provide practice reading appropriate literature and nonfiction text.

About the Units

Each unit is three pages in length. Depending on the needs of your students, you may wish to introduce units in small-group or whole-class settings using a guided-to-independent approach. Reading the passages and responding to activities in collaborative groups allows students to share and support their problem-solving results. As an alternative, students can work independently and compare responses with others. Whichever method you choose, the reading and math activities will provide students with the tools they need to build mathematical knowledge for today's more rigorous math standards.

Page 1

All units begin with a reading passage that presents a mathematical problem or situation. Engaging nonfiction and fiction passages are included in the book. Passages are age-level appropriate and fall within a range of 520 to 820 on the Lexile scale.

Each passage incorporates information to be used for solving practical math problems. They also allow students to experience a variety of genres and make meaningful connections between math and reading.

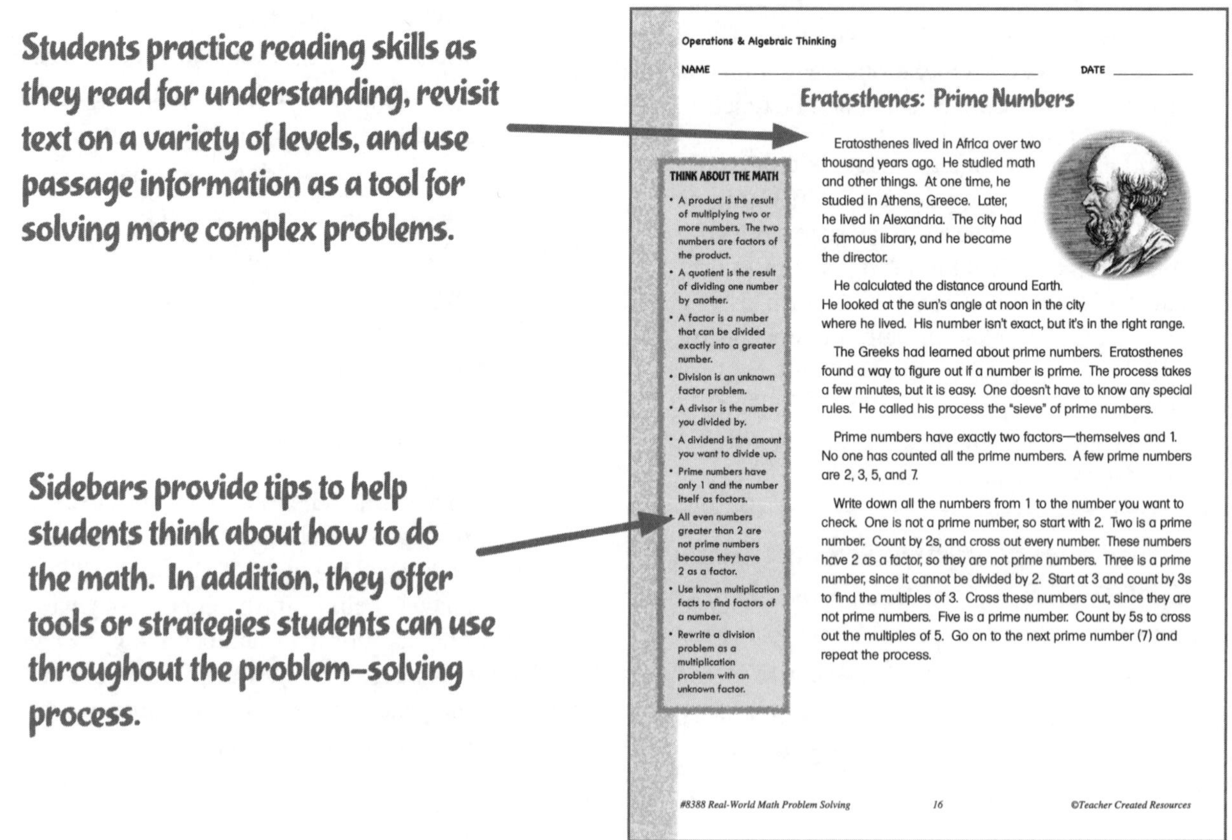

Operations & Algebraic Thinking

NAME ______________________ DATE __________

Eratosthenes: Prime Numbers

Eratosthenes lived in Africa over two thousand years ago. He studied math and other things. At one time, he studied in Athens, Greece. Later, he lived in Alexandria. The city had a famous library, and he became the director.

He calculated the distance around Earth. He looked at the sun's angle at noon in the city where he lived. His number isn't exact, but it's in the right range.

The Greeks had learned about prime numbers. Eratosthenes found a way to figure out if a number is prime. The process takes a few minutes, but it is easy. One doesn't have to know any special rules. He called his process the "sieve" of prime numbers.

Prime numbers have exactly two factors—themselves and 1. No one has counted all the prime numbers. A few prime numbers are 2, 3, 5, and 7.

Write down all the numbers from 1 to the number you want to check. One is not a prime number, so start with 2. Two is a prime number. Count by 2s, and cross out every number. These numbers have 2 as a factor, so they are not prime numbers. Three is a prime number, since it cannot be divided by 2. Start at 3 and count by 3s to find the multiples of 3. Cross these numbers out, since they are not prime numbers. Five is a prime number. Count by 5s to cross out the multiples of 5. Go on to the next prime number (7) and repeat the process.

THINK ABOUT THE MATH

- A product is the result of multiplying two or more numbers. The two numbers are factors of the product.
- A quotient is the result of dividing one number by another.
- A factor is a number that can be divided exactly into a greater number.
- Division is an unknown factor problem.
- A divisor is the number you divided by.
- A dividend is the amount you want to divide up.
- Prime numbers have only 1 and the number itself as factors.
- All even numbers greater than 2 are not prime numbers because they have 2 as a factor.
- Use known multiplication facts to find factors of a number.
- Rewrite a division problem as a multiplication problem with an unknown factor.

#8388 Real-World Math Problem Solving 16 ©Teacher Created Resources

How to Use This Book *(cont.)*

About the Units *(cont.)*

Page 2

The second page of each unit introduces problem-solving tasks. Space is provided for students to draw pictures, work out their answers, write equations, show their work, and explain their thinking. Students are asked to use the unit passage to respond to reading content and investigate the text in order to find solutions to the problems on the page.

The questions require students to look back at the text for clues and information that relates to each question. They must then interpret this information in a way that helps them solve each task on the page. In doing so, students learn to support their responses with concrete evidence.

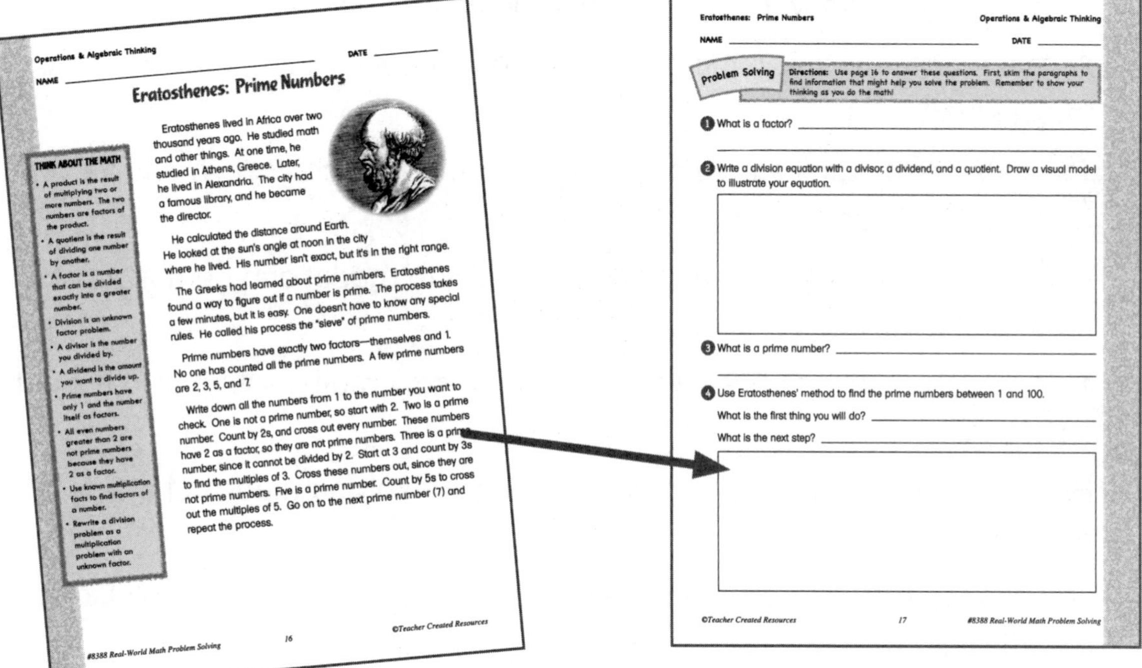

Operations & Algebraic Thinking

NAME ______ DATE ______

Eratosthenes: Prime Numbers

THINK ABOUT THE MATH

- A product is the result of multiplying two or more numbers. The two numbers are factors of the product.
- A quotient is the result of dividing one number by another.
- A factor is a number that can be divided exactly into a greater number.
- Division is an unknown factor problem.
- A divisor is the number you divided by.
- A dividend is the amount you want to divide up.
- Prime numbers have only 1 and the number itself as factors.
- All even numbers greater than 2 are not prime numbers because they have 2 as a factor.
- Use known multiplication facts to find factors of a number.
- Rewrite a division problem as a multiplication problem with an unknown factor.

Eratosthenes lived in Africa over two thousand years ago. He studied math and other things. At one time, he studied in Athens, Greece. Later, he lived in Alexandria. The city had a famous library, and he became the director.

He calculated the distance around Earth. He looked at the sun's angle at noon in the city where he lived. His number isn't exact, but it's in the right range.

The Greeks had learned about prime numbers. Eratosthenes found a way to figure out if a number is prime. The process takes a few minutes, but it is easy. One doesn't have to know any special rules. He called his process the "sieve" of prime numbers.

Prime numbers have exactly two factors—themselves and 1. No one has counted all the prime numbers. A few prime numbers are 2, 3, 5, and 7.

Write down all the numbers from 1 to the number you want to check. One is not a prime number, so start with 2. Two is a prime number. Count by 2s, and cross out every number. These numbers have 2 as a factor, so they are not prime numbers. Three is a prime number, since it cannot be divided by 2. Start at 3 and count by 3s to find the multiples of 3. Cross these numbers out, since they are not prime numbers. Five is a prime number. Count by 5s to cross out the multiples of 5. Go on to the next prime number (7) and repeat the process.

#8388 Real-World Math Problem Solving 16 ©Teacher Created Resources

Eratosthenes: Prime Numbers Operations & Algebraic Thinking

NAME ______ DATE ______

Problem Solving Directions: Use page 16 to answer these questions. First, skim the paragraphs to find information that might help you solve the problem. Remember to show your thinking as you do the math!

1. What is a factor? ______
2. Write a division equation with a divisor, a dividend, and a quotient. Draw a visual model to illustrate your equation.
3. What is a prime number? ______
4. Use Eratosthenes' method to find the prime numbers between 1 and 100.

   What is the first thing you will do? ______

   What is the next step? ______

©Teacher Created Resources 17 #8388 Real-World Math Problem Solving

Page 3

The *Engage* option extends the mathematical situation with questions that allow students to look back at the reading passage and use critical-thinking skills.

The activities in this section strengthen students' comprehension skills by posing questions or situations for which further reflection of the text is required. Questions may be open-ended and require higher-level thinking skills and supported responses. Activities in this section focus on a combination of reading and math skills.

While students can respond independently to the activities on this page, you may wish to have them discuss their answers with a partner, in a small group, or with the entire class. This method can also provide closure to the unit.

Operations & Algebraic Thinking Eratosthenes: Prime Numbers

NAME ______ DATE ______

Engage Directions: Factors are numbers we multiply together to get a product. We use prime numbers to find factors of numbers. This helps us work with fractions. Practice by creating problems with factors and prime numbers.

1. What are the factors of 9? ______

   Is 9 a prime number? ______
2. Is 15 a prime number? ______

   Show how you know.
3. Write two math problems with prime numbers for a classmate to solve.

   What are the factors of the numbers that are the answers for your problems?
4. Codes are used to make information sent over the Internet more secure. It is easy to break a code once you know the pattern. People use prime numbers for codes. Prime numbers do not have a pattern, which makes codes harder to break. Most codes have symbols or numbers, one for each letter of the alphabet. Some codes are shorter. They use numbers like a password.

   Create a code using prime numbers and other symbols. Explain how someone could use your code or write a secret message for a classmate.

#8388 Real-World Math Problem Solving 18 ©Teacher Created Resources

The Path to Common Core Success: A Parent's Guide

Your child's success is measured by much more than numbers or grades. Being successful includes feeling confident and gaining practical skills to help students in life. The following tips will help you work with your child at home to understand the mathematics he or she is learning at school.

- Attend any curriculum or math-coaching nights offered by the school.
- Become familiar with the Standards for Mathematical Practice, which explain how students should apply math concepts and principles.
- Become familiar with the mathematical content standards, which explain what students should know about math and be able to do.
- Ask your child to explain the underlying concept of a math problem or the "main idea."
- Talk together about the core concept of a mathematical task to ensure your child understands it.
- Encourage your child to use concrete objects to model and demonstrate math problems.
- Talk with your child and help him or her to restate math problems in his or her own words.
- Have your child teach you one new strategy for solving a particular type of math problem.
- Discuss (parents and children) how a given strategy might be helpful to solve a particular problem.
- Discuss different ways a problem could be solved.
- Encourage your child to check that his or her solution is accurate and makes sense.
- Talk about ways math rules and concepts apply to specific problems.
- Explain how you used math that day at work or in your daily life.
- Help your child make connections between the day's homework and real life applications.
- Support your child in the process of learning to think critically and analytically.
- Practice patience together with your child as you work on math together.
- Support your child as he or she develops additional reading skills.

NAME ______________________________ DATE ____________

Smart Shopping

A handful of states have laws against plastic bags. Some laws say stores must charge people for single-use bags. The laws often confuse clerks as well as shoppers. Should stores charge customers to use plastic bags, paper bags, or both? Some cities also have bans on bags.

Many places encourage people to bring their own bags. Stores post signs to remind people. Reusing bags means that not as many will end up in a landfill. Sometimes a plastic bag is thrown into a trash or recycle bin. The wind can catch it and blow it away. It becomes a hazard for animals. Some stores have bins where people can put plastic bags to be recycled.

Another reason to bring reusable bags is that some stores offer a discount. It's only a few cents. Over a year the cost can add up. Cloth bags are sturdy and can be used many times. Wash them after carrying meat or produce. This keeps the bags clean for the next grocery trip. One final benefit is cloth bags allow you to express yourself. Choose prints or a message you like, and enjoy helping the environment!

Some shoppers keep their reusable bags in the car so they're handy. Roll up a bag made of lightweight material and hook it to a keychain.

People who buy one or two items can carry them without a bag. In time, the new habit of bringing reusable bags will be easy to remember.

THINK ABOUT THE MATH

- A product is the total number of objects in *x* number of groups of *y* objects each.
- A product is the result of multiplying two or more numbers.
- A quotient is the number of objects in each share when *x* number of objects are divided equally into *y* number of shares.
- A quotient is the result of dividing one number by another.
- Write an addition equation to describe a picture of equal groups. Then, write a related multiplication equation to find the product.
- Draw pictures to show how to equally divide a group of objects.

NAME ______________________ DATE __________

Problem Solving

Directions: Use page 7 to answer these questions. First, skim the paragraphs to find information that might help you solve the problem. Remember to show your thinking as you do the math!

1. If a store offers a 5¢ discount per reusable bag and a customer has 6 bags, how much will that person save? __________

   Use repeated addition or write an equation.

2. If a person saves 30¢ by using cloth bags each week, how much will he save in 6 weeks? Think about place value and multiples of ten to find the answer. __________

   What do we call the answer to these types of equations? __________

3. A customer buys 28 items at the store. She brought 4 bags. Find the quotient when 28 items are divided equally into 4 bags.

   ____

   Draw a picture of the bags and divide the total items equally among the number of bags.

4. The customer in checkout line A has 48 items. She brought 6 bags. The customer in checkout line B has 42 items. He brought 7 bags. If divided equally, which customer will have more items per bag?

   ____

   Draw pictures and write equations to find the quotient when each customer divides their items equally in their bags. Use symbols to stand for unknown numbers.

   Write and label a comparison statement to show which customer has more items in his or her bag.

NAME ______________________________ DATE ____________

Engage **Directions:** Complete each task as directed.

Save More: 5¢
Special Foods: 10¢
Shop 4 Less: 5¢
Food Deals: 5¢

1. Compare the savings for using cloth bags at various grocery stores using the information on the right.

   If you have 7 bags, how much money will you save at Food Deals? ________________

   Draw a picture to show how to find the answer.

   Compare the amount of money saved at Food Deals with 7 bags to the amount of money saved at Special Foods with 7 bags.

2. Think about the food your family buys at the store each week. How many grocery bags do you need? ____________________

3. Think about the store where your family shops. Do they offer a discount for using your own bags? If they do, how much is the discount? If not, how much do you think they should offer per bag?

   ____

4. Describe what the expression 10 × 7 would represent in question 1 above. ________

   ____

   ____

5. Describe what the expression 35 ÷ 5 would represent in question 1 above. ________

   ____

   ____

NAME ______________________________ DATE ____________

Cycling for a Medal

THINK ABOUT THE MATH

- We use multiplication and division to solve word problems involving equal groups.
- There are 60 minutes in an hour.
- Use visual models to divide groups of objects into equal shares.
- Use a letter in place of an unknown number in an equation.
- Rewrite a division problem as a multiplication problem with an unknown factor.
- Round numbers to get an estimate of the correct answer.

Cycling is a popular Olympic Games event. Road cycling has been part of the Olympic Games for over 100 years. Riders race on teams of 4 women or 5 men. The race takes place on public roads. The course covers a distance of 5 to 25 miles. Individual time trials also take place on public roads. In this event, riders race against the clock. The best time wins.

Another category in the Olympic Games is track cycling. There are 5 events: sprint, keirin, team sprint, team pursuit, and omnium. In sprint races, cyclists compete for speed over a short distance. In keirin races, a motorized bike sets the pace for the first part of the race. Then the derny pulls off the track. Cyclists race the remaining 600 meters in a mass sprint of speed. Three-man teams compete in the team sprint. They race 3 laps or a total of 750 meters. In team pursuit, riders race against the clock and other teams. The omnium race combines several different events. Riders receive point scores at the end of each event. The lowest total point score wins.

Many of the events have heats in which cyclists compete for the starting position for semi-finals and final races.

NAME ______________________ DATE ____________

Problem Solving

Directions: Use page 10 to answer these questions. First, skim the paragraphs to find information that might help you solve the problem. Remember to show your thinking as you do the math!

1. An Olympic Games road race can have 150 riders. How many teams of men compete? ____________

   Write an equation with a symbol(s) for the unknown number.

2. Some Olympic Games road races have as many as 180 cyclists. In this case, how many teams of women would compete? ____________

   Write an equation with a symbol(s) for the unknown number.

3. The men's route was just over 150 miles. Medal winners completed the distance in 5 hours and 45 minutes. Round their time to the nearest time in hours. ________

   About how many miles per hour did they ride? ____________

   Draw a visual model—for example, a number line. Divide your visual model into groups based on the number of hours it took riders to complete the race.

4. Use your visual model to write an equation with a symbol for the missing number.

5. Marianne Vos took gold in London 2012. Her time was 3 hours and 35 minutes. How many total minutes did it take her to complete the race? ________

   The women's course was over 80 miles long. If the winner had a speed of 20 miles per hour, how long would it take her to finish the race? ____________

   Compare the gold medalist's actual race time to your answer. What can you tell about her actual race speed?

   ____

NAME ______________________________ DATE ____________

Engage

Directions: Create a track around the classroom or mark off part of the playground to complete the activities below.

1. Measure the distance around the track. Which standard measurement unit makes the most sense to use—centimeters, inches, meters, feet, or yards?

   ____

   Draw and label a picture of the track.

2. Plan races in which people compete in teams or against the clock. Racers may walk, skip, crawl, run, or do another appropriate activity to complete the distance around the track. Describe your race below.

   ____

   ____

   ____

   ____

3. Record the times of racers. Write equations to show the time it took them to travel increments of the total distance.

   ____

   ____

   ____

   Use a visual model to show what happened during the races.

NAME ______________________ DATE __________

Turf and Tree Farms

Trees, grass, and bushes are often planted around new buildings. This is called landscaping. It makes the building look nice. It also keeps the area cool in the summer, which saves energy.

People buy plants at nurseries or farms. It may sound strange, but some trees and grass are grown on farms. The grass is called sod. It is sold in regular rolls and big rolls.

Many turf farms also sell trees. The trees grow in rows similar to other crops. Some places harvest trees from fall through early spring. This is when the trees are dormant. This means they are not actively growing during that time. Some tree farms sell shade trees. There are tree farms that sell only Christmas trees.

Customers buy trees for shade around homes, schools, and businesses. Farmers buy trees to plant as a windbreak on their farms. This helps prevent soil erosion. Trees are planted as needed in parks or other outdoor recreation areas such as golf courses. Trees and grass both make outdoor spaces more enjoyable for people.

THINK ABOUT THE MATH

- A product is the result of multiplying two or more numbers.
- We use multiplication and division to solve problems involving equal groups.
- Area is an attribute of plane figures.
- A square with a side length of 1 unit is equal to 1 square unit of area.
- Area is measured in square units.
- Write an addition equation to describe a visual model. Refer to your addition equation to write an equation to find the product.
- Use an array to solve a problem involving equal groups.
- Draw an array as a visual model to find the product of two numbers.
- Use a letter in place of an unknown number in an equation.

NAME ______________________ DATE ____________

Problem Solving

Directions: Use page 13 to answer these questions. First, skim the paragraphs to find information that might help you solve the problem. Remember to show your thinking as you do the math!

1. A regular-size roll of sod is 2 ft. × 5 ft. How many square feet are in the roll? ________

   If a customer buys 8 rolls, how many sq. ft. will the sod cover? ____________

   Draw a picture to represent the problem.

2. A tree farm has 56 birch trees planted in 8 rows. How many trees are in each row? Write an equation with a symbol for the unknown number.

3. A tree farm wants to plant 10 trees in each row. The farm has 107 Red Oak trees. How many full rows of Red Oak trees will they plant? How many trees are in the incomplete row?

   ____

   Draw an array to find the number of rows of trees planted.

4. Some tree farms have 30 trees in each row. If there are 4 rows of maple trees and one more row with 24 maple trees, how many maple trees does the tree farm have in all?

   ____

NAME ______________________________ DATE ____________

Engage

Directions: Make your own turf and tree farm with craft sticks or twigs and rectangles of green paper. "Plant" the sticks in modeling clay, dirt, or sand to represent trees. Cut and roll the green paper to represent sod.

Draw and label a picture of your model.

1. What things do turf farms need to consider when they haul rolls of sod to a customer?

____

____

2. If a tree farm wants to plant an equal number of trees in each row, why might there be some "left over," as in question 4 on page 14?

____

____

3. What types of trees do you think you could plant closer together on your tree farm?

____

4. Poplars can be planted six feet apart as a windbreak. "Plant" sticks in an array to show a windbreak that is 48 feet long and 3 rows wide.

   Draw a picture of your model.

   How many trees will you need to make the windbreak? ____________

5. Describe what kind of tree you would plant on a tree farm and how many you would like to grow. Who would buy your trees?

____

____

NAME ______________________ DATE ____________

Eratosthenes: Prime Numbers

THINK ABOUT THE MATH

- A product is the result of multiplying two or more numbers. The two numbers are factors of the product.
- A quotient is the result of dividing one number by another.
- A factor is a number that can be divided exactly into a greater number.
- Division is an unknown factor problem.
- A divisor is the number you divided by.
- A dividend is the amount you want to divide up.
- Prime numbers have only 1 and the number itself as factors.
- All even numbers greater than 2 are not prime numbers because they have 2 as a factor.
- Use known multiplication facts to find factors of a number.
- Rewrite a division problem as a multiplication problem with an unknown factor.

Eratosthenes lived in Africa over two thousand years ago. He studied math and other things. At one time, he studied in Athens, Greece. Later, he lived in Alexandria. The city had a famous library, and he became the director.

He calculated the distance around Earth. He looked at the sun's angle at noon in the city where he lived. His number isn't exact, but it's in the right range.

The Greeks had learned about prime numbers. Eratosthenes found a way to figure out if a number is prime. The process takes a few minutes, but it is easy. One doesn't have to know any special rules. He called his process the "sieve" of prime numbers.

Prime numbers have exactly two factors—themselves and 1. No one has counted all the prime numbers. A few prime numbers are 2, 3, 5, and 7.

Write down all the numbers from 1 to the number you want to check. One is not a prime number, so start with 2. Two is a prime number. Count by 2s, and cross out every number. These numbers have 2 as a factor, so they are not prime numbers. Three is a prime number, since it cannot be divided by 2. Start at 3 and count by 3s to find the multiples of 3. Cross these numbers out, since they are not prime numbers. Five is a prime number. Count by 5s to cross out the multiples of 5. Go on to the next prime number (7) and repeat the process.

NAME ______________________ DATE __________

Problem Solving

Directions: Use page 16 to answer these questions. First, skim the paragraphs to find information that might help you solve the problem. Remember to show your thinking as you do the math!

1. What is a factor? ______________________

____

2. Write a division equation with a divisor, a dividend, and a quotient. Draw a visual model to illustrate your equation.

3. What is a prime number? ______________________

____

4. Use Eratosthenes' method to find the prime numbers between 1 and 100.

What is the first thing you will do? ______________________

What is the next step? ______________________

NAME ______________________________ DATE ____________

Engage

Directions: Factors are numbers we multiply together to get a product. We use prime numbers to find factors of numbers. This helps us work with fractions. Practice by creating problems with factors and prime numbers.

1. What are the factors of 9? ______________________________

   Is 9 a prime number? ____________

2. Is 15 a prime number?

   ____

   Show how you know.

3. Write two math problems with prime numbers for a classmate to solve.

   What are the factors of the numbers that are the answers for your problems?

   ____

4. Codes are used to make information sent over the Internet more secure. It is easy to break a code once you know the pattern. People use prime numbers for codes. Prime numbers do not have a pattern, which makes codes harder to break. Most codes have symbols or numbers, one for each letter of the alphabet. Some codes are shorter. They use numbers like a password.

   Create a code using prime numbers and other symbols. Explain how someone could use your code or write a secret message for a classmate.

   ____

   ____

   ____

NAME ______________________________ DATE ____________

Seven Times One

by Jean Ingelow

There's no dew left on the daisies and clover,
There's no rain left in heaven.
I've said my "seven times" over and over,
Seven times one are seven.

I am old, so old, I can write a letter;
My birthday lessons are done;
The lambs play always, they know no better;
They are only one times one.

O moon! In the night I have seen you sailing
And shining so round and low;
You were bright! Ah bright! But your light is failing—
You are nothing now but a bow.

You moon, have you done something wrong in heaven
That God has hidden your face?
I hope, if you have, you will soon be forgiven,
And shine again in your place.

O velvet bee, you're a dusty fellow,
You've powdered your legs with gold!
O brave marsh marybuds, rich and yellow,
Give me your money to hold!

O columbine, open your folded wrapper,
Where two twin turtle-doves dwell!
O cuckoo pint, toll me the purple clapper
That hangs in your clear green bell!

And show me your nest with the young ones in it;
I will not steal them away;
I am old! you may trust me, linnet, linnet—
I am seven times one to-day.

THINK ABOUT THE MATH

- It does not matter in which order two numbers are multiplied.
- Use letters to stand for unknown numbers.
- There are patterns in addition and multiplication.
- Use patterns in multiplication to solve problems.
- Use a hundreds chart to see patterns in multiplication.

NAME ______________________ DATE __________

Problem Solving

Directions: Use page 19 to answer these questions. First, skim the poem to find information that might help you solve the problem. Remember to show your thinking as you do the math!

1. Copy the math sentence in the first stanza.

____

____

Write an equation using numbers and symbols to express this sentence.

What is another way to write this equation?

2. Write equations to show the "seven times" multiplication facts. Write each fact two ways.

What is true about $n \times 7$ and $7 \times n$? ______________________

3. What other multiplication facts could help you remember the "seven times" facts?

____

4. Use numbers and symbols to write an equation that shows how old the lambs are.

5. Write equations to show the "one times" facts.

NAME ______________________ DATE __________

Engage **Directions:** Think about what is happening in the poem and discuss with classmates.

1. How old is the person talking in this poem? __________ Explain how you know.

____

____

2. What is the occasion for the poem? ______________________

____

3. What can the author do now? ______________________

____

4. Circle any words you do not know. Work with a classmate to find the meanings for these words.

5. What things does the author see on this special day? Use words and pictures to describe what the author sees.

NAME ______________________ DATE __________

The Ski Jump

THINK ABOUT THE MATH

- You can use multiplication or division to find the unknown number in some equations.
- When multiplying two numbers, it does not matter in which order they are multiplied.
- If two numbers and an operation symbol are in parentheses, do the operation for those numbers first.
- Use letters to stand for unknown numbers in an equation.
- Use rounding to quickly estimate the correct answer.
- Draw a picture when needed to understand what is happening in a problem.

"The slopes are great today here in the Alps! Head on over to the ski jump and give it a try!" An announcement came over the loud speaker.

"There are skiers here from all over planet Og to try this ski jump. Let's hurry before the line gets too long." Zargo tugged on Ezkra's arm.

"How much does it cost?" She tagged along behind him.

"The gate man makes it simple to figure out. He charges residents 3 dollars per ski and 4 dollars per pole. Anyone who wants to jump needs 1 ski per foot and 1 pole per arm."

Zargo and Ezkra arrived at the gate to find three others standing in line before them. When it was their turn, the gate man counted Zargo's 3 feet and 6 arms. "Welcome! You're going to have a great day!" He took Zargo's money and waved him through.

"Do you have your protective gear?" He peered at Ezkra.

"What do I need?" The fur covering her entire body muffled her voice in the wind.

"Skis and poles! You have 2 arms and 2 feet, and it's 3 dollars per ski and 4 dollars per pole."

"What about these?" Ezkra swished her 3 tails.

The gate man grinned. "Those go free."

They strapped on their skis and hopped onto the lift. As it started to move, Ezkra pointed to the gate. "Look how long the line is now!"

Zargo said, "There are 74 people in line."

"How did you count that quickly?"

"Easy, I counted by 5s and then 2s."

They finished their run and glided to a stop beyond the gate. "Let's go again!" Ezkra exclaimed.

NAME ______________________ DATE __________

Problem Solving

Directions: Use page 22 to answer these questions. First, skim the paragraphs to find information that might help you solve the problem. Remember to show your thinking as you do the math!

1. How much did Zargo pay to jump?

   How much did Ezkra give the gate man?

   How much more did Zargo pay?

2. The creature behind Ezkra paid $32. He had 4 feet. How many arms did he have?

3. If Zargo goes on 2 runs, how much will his day of skiing cost?

   If Ezkra goes on 2 runs, how much will her day of skiing cost?

4. Most creatures that go through the gate pay at least $15. If Zargo's count is correct, how much money will the gate man collect? Round numbers to the nearest 10 to estimate your answer.

   Check your estimate. Use properties of numbers to write equations to find the exact answer.

NAME ______________________________ DATE ____________

Engage

Directions: Research with classmates to learn about a popular activity in your area. It might be a sport like skiing. It could be renting a boat or a bicycle. It might be visiting the zoo or a swimming pool.

1. What is the cost per ticket of the place you researched? ____________

   How much would it cost for a group of 10 people to do this activity? ____________

   ____

2. What special gear or equipment does a person need to do the activity you read about?

   ____

   ____

   ____

3. What are some reasons sports and activities have special gear?

   ____

   ____

   ____

4. What are some factors that affect which activities people choose?

   ____

   ____

   ____

5. Write about an experience you have had doing an activity. How did math play a role in the activity?

   ____

   ____

   ____

   ____

   ____

NAME ______________________________ DATE ____________

Catch the Next Train

Madison wiggled to get comfortable on the couch between her cousins. The boys had spread a glossy brochure across their laps.

"This says they have a new insect exhibit at the zoo." Nolan pointed to a picture of a caterpillar.

"I vote for the space museum!" Ethan bounced his feet, nearly knocking the brochure to the floor.

Madison studied the pictures. "This city park might have a cool playground structure." She traced the colored line with her finger. "What does each color mean?"

"It shows which light rail line goes each direction," Grandma said.

Nolan folded the edge of the brochure over to look at the back. "There are a lot of different trains. Red, green, blue, orange, yellow—even brown!"

Grandpa unfolded another brochure. "And they all have different schedules. Here, you kids can help me make sense of this. The orange train leaves every 4 minutes, and the red train leaves every 5 minutes. You have to wait 10 minutes between brown trains. Make a table with colored pencils or crayons, so we can figure out what time to get to the station and how long we might have to wait."

"Don't we need to know which train we want?" Nolan asked.

"Yes," Grandma said. "But if we miss one train and don't want to wait for another train, we might be able to take a different train and transfer."

"Too confusing," Grandpa said. "Make a chart."

THINK ABOUT THE MATH

- When multiplying two numbers, it does not matter in which order they are multiplied.
- There are 60 minutes in an hour.
- Use patterns in multiplication to solve problems.
- Use patterns (odd or even factors and products) to check that your answer makes sense.
- Use skip counting to remember multiplication facts.

NAME ______________________________ DATE ______________

Problem Solving

Directions: Use page 25 to answer these questions. First, skim the paragraphs to find information that might help you solve the problem. Remember to show your thinking as you do the math!

1. The cousins made a chart similar to the one shown below. Use information from the reading passage, multiplication facts, or skip counting to complete the chart. The first train has been done for you.

	Yellow	Orange	Red	Green	Blue	Silver	Brown
Depart main terminal	12:00	12:00	12:00	12:00	12:00	12:00	12:00
Frequency	3 min.	4 min.	5 min.	7 min.	8 min.	9 min.	10 min.
Train 1	12:03	12:04	12:05	12:07	12:08	12:09	12:10
Train 2							
Train 3							
Train 4							
Train 5							
Train 6							
Train 7							
Train 8							
Train 9							
Train 10							

2. There is construction on the yellow train line that causes delays. To keep the trains from backing up, they are running only every other train. What is the amount of time between trains with the change in schedule? ______________

On the backside of this page, make a table or list to show the times the yellow line will run.

3. Which increments of minutes from 1 to 10 are not shown on this train table? ____________

4. If Trains 1 through 10 run constantly all day, when will Train 1 come back around again on the red line? ______________

NAME ______________________ DATE ____________

Engage **Directions:** Complete each task as directed.

1. Color the column for each train lightly with the color that describes that train.

2. What mathematical relationship can you find between the train numbers and the minutes listed in many of the departure times?

____

____

3. Which operation do you think is more helpful to use to figure out the departure times—multiplication or division? Explain.

____

____

____

4. Use the chart on page 26 to write math questions for classmates to practice using multiplication facts.

____

____

____

____

____

____

____

____

____

____

____

NAME ______________________ DATE ____________

Modern Medicine Helps People

Polio is a disease that used to be common in the United States. Caused by a virus, it affected more children than adults. In most people, the virus resulted in symptoms like the flu. In a few people, though, the virus attacked the nervous system. Those people became paralyzed.

In 1953, Dr. Jonas Salk developed a polio vaccine. It would protect people against the three major strains of the virus. This vaccine used inactive (killed) viruses. It is very safe because people do not get sick from the dead viruses. This type of vaccine comes in the form of a shot.

Later, Albert Sabin developed a different polio vaccine. It used live viruses that were weak. This vaccine came in the form of a pill people could swallow. It was cheaper to make, so it was used in some places.

During the worst years before the vaccine, there were many cases of polio. In 1916, in New York City alone, 9,000 people had polio. Of those, 2,343 died. In the country overall there were 27,000 cases in 1916. At least 6,000 people died. In the years between 1949 and 1954, 35 out of every 100 people with polio were adults.

In 2014, there were no cases of polio in the United States. Modern medicine has helped prevent this and other diseases over the last 100 years.

THINK ABOUT THE MATH

- The digit to the left of the ones shows how many tens are in a number.
- The digit to the left of the tens shows how many hundreds are in a number.
- If the ones are equal to or greater than 5, round up to the next 10.
- If the tens are equal to or greater than 5, round up to the next 100.
- The digit to the left of the hundreds place shows how many thousands are in a number.
- Hundreds and thousands are separated by a comma in a number.
- There are 10 groups of 10 in 100.
- There are 10 groups of 100 in 1,000.
- Look at the ones place to round numbers to the nearest 10.
- Look at the tens place to round numbers to the nearest 100.
- Group by tens or hundreds to add or subtract numbers up to 1,000.

NAME ______________________________ DATE ____________

Problem Solving

Directions: Use page 28 to answer these questions. First, skim the paragraphs to find information that might help you solve the problem. Remember to show your thinking as you do the math!

1. How many years has it been since Dr. Salk developed a vaccine for polio? Round each year to the nearest 10 to estimate an answer. ____________

   Write an equation and find the exact number of years.

2. In 1916, how many people in New York City survived polio? Round the number of people who did not survive in New York City to the nearest 100 to estimate an answer.

   ____

   Write an equation and find the exact number of people who survived.

3. In that same year, how many more cases were in the rest of the United States outside of New York City? ____________

   How many people survived in the United States? ____________

4. Draw a number line from 0 to 100. Divide it into 10 equal parts. Label each interval of 10. Mark the place on the number line that represents the number of adults with polio out of every 100 cases of the illness, between 1949 and 1954. Write a fraction to show what part of every 100 cases of polio was an adult.

NAME ______________________ DATE __________

Engage **Directions:** Use rounding and place-value strategies to answer the questions.

1. Today in the United States, most children get vaccines to protect themselves against polio. Doctors suggest 4 doses of polio vaccine in children. Most vaccines are in the form of shots. Children get a shot at ages 2 months and 4 months. They get the third shot between age 6–18 months. There is a booster shot before the child starts school, sometime between 4–6 years old.

   How many children are in your class? ______________________

   How many third-grade classes are in your school? ______________________

   About how many third graders total are in your school? ______________________

   Round to the nearest 10. ______________________

2. If getting fully vaccinated, how many polio vaccines does each child receive? ______

   How many total polio vaccines would be needed for the third graders in your school (use the rounded number)? ______________

   Use place-value strategies, properties of multiplication, or group by tens to find the total number of vaccines given.

3. How many years after the 1916 polio epidemic did Dr. Salk develop his vaccine? ______

4. How many years were there between the 1947 cases and the 1916 cases? ________

5. How many deaths in 1916 were outside of New York City? ______________________

   Write an equation. Use addition to check your answer.

NAME ______________________________ DATE ____________

Full of Life*

Full of life, now, compact, visible,
I, forty years old the Eighty-third Year of The States,
To one a century hence, or any number of centuries hence,
To you, yet unborn, these, seeking you.

When you read these, I, that was visible, am become invisible;
Now it is you, compact, visible, realizing my poems, seeking me;
Fancying how happy you were, if I could be with you, and
become your comrade;
Be it as if I were with you. (Be not too certain but I am now
with you.)

THINK ABOUT THE MATH

- The digit to the left of the ones place shows how many tens are in a number.
- The digit to the left of the tens place shows how many hundreds are in a number.
- The digit to the left of the hundreds place shows how many thousands are in a number.
- There are 10 groups of 10 in 100.
- There are 10 groups of 100 in 1,000.
- Look at the ones place to round numbers to the nearest 10.
- If the digit in the ones place is 5 or greater, round up to the nearest 10.
- If the digit in the tens place is 5 or greater, round up to the nearest 100.
- Group by tens or hundreds to add or subtract numbers up to 1,000.

*from *Leaves of Grass* by Walt Whitman (adapted)

NAME ______________________ DATE __________

Problem Solving

Directions: Use page 31 to answer these questions. First, skim the poem to find information that might help you solve the problem. Remember to show your thinking as you do the math!

1. The United States declared independence from Great Britain in 1776. In what year is the narrator speaking? __________

   How could this be written as a subtraction problem?

2. How old is the speaker in the poem? __________

   In what year was the speaker born? __________

3. How many years are in a century? __________

4. *Hence* means from now. What year would be one century from the time of the poem? __________

5. Write an equation to show how many more years than a century have passed since the time of the poem. Use letters to stand for unknown numbers.

   Did you write an addition or subtraction equation to find the number of years over a century? Why did you choose to write that type of equation?

   ____

   Round your answer to the nearest 10 years. __________

   Has it been closer to one or two centuries since the time of the poem? __________

6. How many years has it been since the narrator spoke? Round your answer to the nearest 10 years. __________

NAME ______________________ DATE __________

Engage **Directions:** Think about the poem and its view of time. Then, answer the questions below.

1. What does it mean when the speaker says he "was visible"? ______________________

____

2. Who is visible in the second stanza? ______________________

What is happening in the second stanza when the poet says he is invisible? ______

____

3. Describe one thing you know about something from a century ago. ______________________

____

4. The poet sees a link between his writing and those who will read this poem in the future. Now that you have read the poem, what is one comment you have about it?

____

____

5. What is one thing you would like to say to people who might read your writing in the future?

____

____

6. Write a poem about something that is important to you. Share your poem with classmates.

____

____

____

____

____

____

NAME ______________________________ DATE ______________

Small Town U.S.A.: Walpi, Arizona

THINK ABOUT THE MATH

- The digit to the left of the tens place shows how many hundreds are in a number.
- The digit to the left of the hundreds place shows how many thousands are in a number.
- There are 10 groups of 10 in 100.
- There are 10 groups of 100 in 1,000.
- Look at the ones place to round numbers to the nearest 10.
- Look at the tens place to round numbers to the nearest 100.
- Group by tens or hundreds to add or subtract numbers up to 1,000.
- Use addition to check subtraction.

On the high desert of Arizona, native people have lived for hundreds of years. First Mesa is an area on the Hopi reservation. There are three villages within this area. A total of 1,124 people live within the villages. The 2010 census lists a total population of 7,185 for the Hopi reservation.

The main part of the village of Walpi is at a 6,181-foot elevation. The village in the valley below is at a 5,810-foot elevation. People there say the village has been lived in for 900 years. This makes Walpi the oldest of the three villages.

Springs on the mesas provide water. People also made depressions in the earth to collect rainwater. In the past, the 600-foot cliffs on the sides of the narrow mesas discouraged enemies. At its narrowest point, the mesa is 15 feet wide.

Today, stone houses still stand, blending in with the environment. Hopi have been described as cliff dwellers. They practiced dry farming. This includes observing where sagebrush grows heaviest. There will be more natural moisture in the ground in that place. They also keep gardens and fields clear from weeds. The weeds take moisture away from the plants they want to grow.

Visitors may tour Walpi with a guide. The walking tour has a route of less than one mile. The trail begins at 6,214-feet elevation and gains a total of 10 feet in height.

NAME ______________________________ DATE ____________

Problem Solving

Directions: Use page 34 to answer these questions. First, skim the paragraphs to find information that might help you solve the problem. Remember to show your thinking as you do the math!

1. How many people on the Hopi reservation do not live on First Mesa?

____

Round each number to the nearest 100 and do this problem again. Then, write an addition equation to check your work.

2. What is the distance in elevation between the main part of Walpi and the village on the valley floor? ____________

Round each number to the nearest 100 and do this problem again. Then, write an addition equation to check your work.

3. What elevation might be the highest point on the walking trail? ____________

4. How many years have people lived in the village of Walpi? ____________

In what year might people have first settled in the village? ____________

5. Some sources say the first European settlers landed in the Americas in 1492. Based on your answer to question 4, how many years might this have been after the settlement of Walpi?

____

NAME ______________________________ DATE ____________

Engage

Directions: Think about life on the reservation. Use brochures, local library resources, or the Internet to answer some of the questions below.

1. Find the elevation of your town. How does your town differ from the village of Walpi in elevation? ______________________________

____

Write an equation to show the difference in elevation.

Write a sentence to describe what the elevation difference might mean. ____________

____

2. Find the population of your town. How does it differ from the village of Walpi? ____________

____

Write an equation to show the difference in population.

Write a sentence to explain the population difference. ______________________________

____

3. One lane of a ~~public~~ road in the United States is 9 to 12 feet wide. The street in front of your school is most likely two lanes, or a minimum of 20 feet wide.

How many lanes are on the road in front of your school? ______________________________

What would you guess is the width of the road? ______________________________

What is the difference between the width of the mesa and the width of the road in front of your school? ______________________________

NAME ______________________ **DATE** __________

Problem Solving

Directions: Use page 40 to answer these questions. First, skim the paragraphs to find information that might help you solve the problem. Remember to show your thinking as you do the math!

1. A line of type in the passage you read has space for about 85 characters. About 70 of those characters are letters. How many individual letter blocks would be needed to print one line of type?

   ____

   How many letter blocks would be needed to print 10 lines? ______________

2. Gutenberg's book had 42 lines per page. How many letter blocks might he need to print one page of type? ______________

   Use expanded form to decompose numbers and multiply by multiples of 10.

3. How many more pages a day could Gutenberg's press print than earlier methods? Think about place value to find the difference in the number of pages.

4. About how many copies of the Bible did Gutenberg print each year?

NAME ______________________________ DATE ____________

Engage **Directions:** Think about place value, and then answer the questions below.

1. Count the lines of type in the reading passage on page 40. Round to the nearest 10.

   ____

   If there are 70 letter blocks for one line of type, how many letters blocks would you need to print the reading passage? ____________________

2. How long do you think it would take you to copy the reading passage by hand?

   ____

   The people who set the pages of blocks were called compositors. They put type together by hand. Someone skilled at this job could set 2,000 letters in an hour. If there are about 65 letters per line, about how long would it take a skilled person to set the reading passage to print?

   ____

3. The printer would hand-press the inked letters on one page at a time. Gutenberg could print up to 25 pages an hour. How many copies of the reading passage could he make in one 8-hour day?

   ____

   If your favorite book has 184 pages, how many complete copies could Gutenberg print in one 8-hour day? ____________________

   How many days would it take him to make a copy for everyone in your class to read? ____________________

NAME ______________________________ DATE ____________

A Land of Extremes

Death Valley, California, is known for extremes. The name itself cautions all who visit. It is one of the hottest and driest places on Earth. Summer temperatures average well over 100 degrees. In 1996, the valley experienced 40 days in a row of temperatures over 120 degrees. Five years later, the highs were over 100 degrees for 154 days.

Air tends to be warmer at lower elevations. Death Valley is one of the lowest places on Earth. Furnace Creek is 190 feet below sea level. On a hot day in 1972, the air temperature at Furnace Creek was 128 degrees. The ground temperature that day was 201 degrees. Badwater Basin is even lower in elevation at 282 feet below sea level.

The opposite is also true. Air cools at higher elevations. The air temperature drops as much as 10 degrees for every increase of elevation of 2,000 feet.

In stark contrast, winter low temperatures drop to within 10 degrees of freezing. Death Valley averages less than 2 inches of rain per year. About once every 10 years there might be a light dusting of snow. The highest peak in Death Valley National Park is 11,049 feet in elevation.

All this occurs within a distance of 25 miles. No wonder people call it an extreme place!

THINK ABOUT THE MATH

- Use rounding to quickly check possible answers.
- Use known multiplication facts to multiply multiples of 10.
- Use mental math strategies to find answers to questions when possible.
- Use estimation strategies to check mental math computations.
- Water boils at 212°F.
- Water freezes at 32°F.

NAME ______________________________ DATE ______________

Problem Solving

Directions: Use page 43 to answer these questions. First, skim the paragraphs to find information that might help you solve the problem. Remember to show your thinking as you do the math!

1. The temperature drops 10 degrees for every 2,000 of feet elevation. How much lower is the temperature at 6,000 feet elevation than at sea level? __________

   If the temperature at sea level is 112 degrees, what is the temperature at 6,000 feet elevation? __________

2. How much rain does this driest place in the United States get in an average year?

   ____

   Louisiana receives over 30 times that amount of rainfall in an average year. How many inches does this state get? __________

3. In what year did the valley have 154 days of over 100-degree temperatures? __________

   If there are an average of 30 days in a month, for how many months was the temperature over 100 degrees every day? Round if needed to get an estimate of the correct answer. __________

4. The record high temperature for the valley is 134 degrees on a day in July. Death Valley's record low temperature is 15 degrees, recorded on a cold January day. What is the difference between these two temperature extremes? __________

5. A warm day in Miami, Florida, in the winter was 75 degrees in 2015. How many times warmer is that than the record low temperature in Death Valley? __________

6. What is the freezing temperature of water? __________

   How far below freezing is the record low? __________

   How far above freezing is the record high? __________

   What is the boiling temperature of water? __________

   How close did the ground temperature at Furnace Creek get to the temperature at which water will boil? __________

NAME ______________________ DATE ____________

Engage **Directions:** Look back at the reading passage on page 43. Research and learn more about Death Valley and the climate where you live.

1. Write math problems using information from the previous two pages.

2. Write math problems using high and low temperatures for your town.

3. Look up the amount of rain your town receives and compare it to Death Valley or another location.

4. Create a line plot of rain amounts in different years for your town, Death Valley, or another place.

5. Share your math problems with classmates. In the box below, copy a classmate's interesting problem that you solved.

NAME ______________________ DATE __________

Picking Cotton

THINK ABOUT THE MATH

- There are one hundred pennies in one dollar.
- There are four quarters in one dollar.
- There are ten dimes in one dollar.
- There are twenty nickels in one dollar.
- A fraction shows the number of parts in a whole.
- The numerator in a fraction shows the number of parts being considered.
- The denominator in a fraction shows the total number of equal parts in the whole.
- Compare the numerators and denominators of fractions to determine which fraction describes a larger share.
- Compare fractions that are part of the same whole.
- Use a visual model to compare fractions.
- Equivalent fractions represent the same part of a whole.

I pushed my sunbonnet back and mopped my face. The sun beat down on the cotton, the dirt, and all of us working in the field. I'd heard my parents talking the night before at dinner. Crop prices haven't gone up yet. We'll have to keep working in the neighbor's fields for this season. It takes all of us—my three brothers and sister—to help earn enough money for our family to survive. My name is Emma, and I'm in the middle. Charles, Thomas, and Edward are all older than me. Minnie is only 6, three years younger than me.

Early mornings, it isn't so bad. I like being outside, feeling the soft cotton as I pick it. The sack hangs over my shoulder from a strap. I pull carefully at each cotton boll, to get all of it without getting stabbed with a sharp thorn. When both hands are full, I shove the cotton into the sack.

At noon, a bell rings. We get an hour for our dinner break and rest. Then we work through the afternoon until the final bell at five o'clock. We take our sacks to be weighed. Our pay is one cent per pound. The grownups can pick 200 pounds of cotton in a day. I've never been able to pick more than 100 pounds.

"Hard work never hurt anybody," my father likes to say. And I'm glad I can help our family. We're all in this together.

NAME ______________________ DATE __________

Problem Solving

Directions: Use page 46 to answer these questions. First, skim the paragraphs to find information that might help you solve the problem. Remember to show your thinking as you do the math!

1. How many quarters are in a dollar? ____________

   Emma picked only 75 pounds today. How much money did she earn? ____________

   How many quarters is that? ____________

   What fraction of a dollar does she have? ____________

2. How many dimes are in a dollar? ____________

   Minnie picked 50 pounds. How much money does she have? ____________

   How many dimes is that? ____________

   What fraction of a dollar does she have? ____________

   What is another name for this fraction? ____________

3. How many nickels are in a dollar? ____________

   How many parts are in the whole? Write a fraction to show what part of a dollar one nickel is. ____________

   Everyone in the family gives most of their earnings to their parents. Thomas gets to keep a share of his earnings. He is the oldest and is saving for when he gets out on his own. If Thomas has 5 nickels in his pocket, how much of a whole dollar does he have?

   Write a fraction to show how much money Thomas has. ____________

4. How much money does Thomas have? 5 nickels = ____________

   How much of a dollar is that? Write a fraction to show this number. ____________

5. Does Thomas have the same amount of money in questions 3 and 4? ____________

   What is true about the fractions you wrote in questions 3 and 4? ____________

   ____

   Draw a picture to model your answer and write a sentence to describe your picture.

   ____

   ____

NAME ______________________________ DATE ______________

Engage

Directions: Draw cotton sacks on a separate piece of paper. Label each sack with a number to show how many pounds of cotton are in the sack. Cut out the sacks. Work with classmates in a small group. Have each person select a cotton sack at random. Use pieces of paper or other models to represent coins.

1. How many pounds of cotton are in the sack you received? ______________

2. If you picked that many pounds of cotton in one day, how much money would you earn? ______________

3. What fraction of a dollar did you receive? ______________

4. Combine your money with other people in your "family" group. How much money did everyone earn in all for this day? ______________

5. Draw a picture to show the total amount of money earned.

6. Color parts of your picture to show the fractional amount each person in the group earned out of the whole.

   Write fractions and label each to show which person earned which fraction of the whole.

7. Which fraction represents the greatest amount of the whole? ______________

   Which fraction represents the least amount of the whole? ______________

   Which two people earned the closest to the same amount of the whole?

   ____

NAME ______________________________ DATE ____________

Our Earth: Water and Land

Did you know that about three-quarters of Earth is covered by water? Large areas of water are divided by large masses of land. We call the water *oceans* and the land *continents*.

Those who study geography divide the water into five oceans. The oceans all touch each other. Some people say there is one world ocean. The Pacific Ocean borders the West Coast of the United States. It is the largest ocean and covers one-third of Earth. The Atlantic Ocean is next to the East Coast. The Arctic Ocean is at the North Pole. It is 10 times smaller than the Pacific Ocean. The water between Africa, India, and Australia is called the Indian Ocean. The Southern Ocean circles Antarctica.

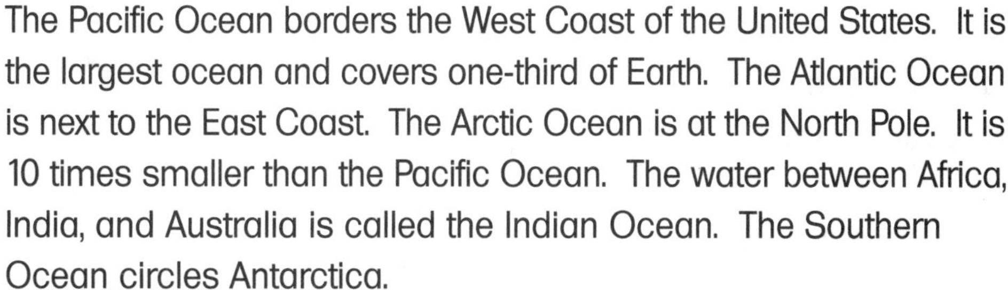

Each land mass has a name. Some continents are connected to each other by land. They are considered separate continents if the people have very different cultures. Europe is a continent, and Asia is a different continent, but they share the same land mass. We live on the continent of North America. South America is a separate continent. Australia is a large island that is considered a continent. Africa is surrounded by water. Antarctica has oceans all around it, so it is also a continent.

Each continent has rivers. The longest river in the world is the Nile River. It flows for over 4,000 miles through Africa. Two rivers are listed as the shortest. The Roe River in Montana is 200 feet long. It flows between a spring and another river. D River in Oregon flows from Devils Lake to the Pacific Ocean. It is 400 feet long, but its length changes with the tides.

There are many other interesting features on each continent. It would take a lifetime to explore them all.

THINK ABOUT THE MATH

- A fraction shows the number of parts in a whole.
- Fractions define parts between 0 and 1 on a number line.
- Equivalent fractions represent the same part of a whole.
- Compare the numerators and denominators of fractions to determine which fraction describes a larger share.
- Identify the total number of equal parts in a whole to divide the segment between 0 and 1 on a number line.
- The numerator of the fraction tells you where the fraction is placed on the number line between 0 and 1.
- Compare fractions that are part of the same whole.
- Use a visual model to compare fractions.

NAME ______________________ DATE __________

Problem Solving

Directions: Use page 49 to answer these questions. First, skim the paragraphs to find information that might help you solve the problem. Remember to show your thinking as you do the math!

1. How many oceans is the water on Earth divided into? ________
   About how much of Earth is covered by water? ________
   Draw a picture to compare the amount of Earth that is ocean with the amount of Earth that is land.

2. Which ocean is the largest?
   ____
   Draw a picture of Earth and shade it to show how much is covered by the largest ocean.
   Which ocean is closest to where you live?
   ____

3. How many continents are on Earth? ________
   Why do some land masses have more than one continent? ________
   ____
   Which two continents are on the same land mass? ________

4. What is the name and length of the longest river in the world? ________
   How much shorter is the Roe River than the D River? ________
   What affects the length of the D River? ________

5. Draw a number line to compare the lengths of the two shortest rivers.

NAME ______________________ DATE ____________

Engage **Directions:** Using classroom or library books or Internet resources, learn more about the continents, countries, and geography of our world.

1. What is one unique feature of North America?

____

____

2. What is the longest river in North America? ____________

   How does it compare with the longest river in the world?

____

3. What is the height of the tallest mountain in North America? ____________

____

4. How can different culture groups live on the same continent?

____

____

____

____

5. Which continent or ocean would you most like to see? Why?

____

____

____

____

____

____

____

____

NAME ________________________ DATE __________

A New Bike Path

THINK ABOUT THE MATH

- A fraction shows the number of parts in a whole.
- The numerator in a fraction shows the number of parts being considered.
- The denominator in a fraction shows the total number of equal parts in the whole.
- Fractions define amounts between 0 and 1 on a number line.
- We can mark distance increments in blocks as well as in parts of a mile.
- Identify the total number of equal parts in one whole to divide the segment between 0 and 1 on a number line.
- Use a ruler to think about line segments greater than one inch.

"May I take my snack to the front steps?" Anton tossed his backpack on the kitchen table. He grabbed the cheese and crackers his aunt had set out. "I want to watch them work on the bike path." He was upset when they first tore up the bike path across the street. But then he saw the sign that said they were making a new bike path.

The first day, big machines trimmed the bushes back to make room to work. Another machine broke up large pieces of the old bike path. Then he'd watched the workers use shovels to level the dirt and gravel. They made a smooth path that was a little wider than the old path.

They put some rock mixed with tar down the next day. It looked like asphalt but didn't make a smooth path. Anton couldn't figure out why they did that.

He watched as a truck dumped piles of hot asphalt along the path. Smoke rose, and the air smelled like burning tar. A smaller machine came behind. It rolled the piles into a smooth path. Anton liked this part. It seemed as though the new path would really happen. He couldn't wait to ride his bike on the new path!

NAME ______________________________ DATE ____________

Engage **Directions:** Compare the two recipes for pancakes. Work with fractions to rewrite the older recipe to use today.

1. List the differences you see between the two recipes.

____

____

____

2. How much of each spice do you think people used in the old recipe? Think about how we measure spices today (e.g., teaspoon, half teaspoon, quarter teaspoon). Use the measurements in the new recipe as a guide.

____

____

____

3. The older recipe from 1615 needs ________ eggs. The more recent recipe from 1956 needs ________ egg. The amount of eggs in the older recipe is ________ times the amount needed in the recipe from 1956.

4. Work with a classmate to double the recipe from 1956. Use addition, multiplication, or a number line to find the amount of each ingredient you will need.

NAME ______________________ DATE ____________

Concrete Everywhere

THINK ABOUT THE MATH

- A fraction shows the number of equal parts in a whole.
- The numerator in a fraction shows the number of equal parts being considered.
- The denominator in a fraction shows the total number of equal parts in the whole.
- Equivalent fractions represent the same part of a whole.
- Equivalent fractions are equal.
- Use a visual fraction model to determine if two fractions are equal.
- Compare fractions that are part of the same whole.
- Compare the numerators and denominators of fractions to determine which fraction describes a larger share.

In a city, it seems everywhere we look we see concrete. Buildings, sidewalks, and bridges are all made of cement or concrete. Sometimes we use these words to mean the same thing. But cement and concrete are made differently.

Cement is made of lime, which comes from limestone. Limestone has calcium in it. The stone is burned, and the leftover ash is lime. Lime is mixed with dry clay to make cement. Clay is sticky, fine-grained dirt. Add water, and it becomes soft dough. When the cement dries, it becomes hard. People build many structures with cement.

Concrete is a stronger building material. We make concrete by mixing cement with sand and gravel. Start with two pounds of cement. Add four pounds of sand. Stir in six pounds of crushed rock or gravel. Finally, add two pounds of water to make a paste. It takes a little less than two cups of water to make one pound.

People use these small amounts to make concrete for a patio or walkway at their house. You might see a truck pouring cement for a new sidewalk in town. Once it dries, cement or concrete becomes a hard surface that will last in all kinds of weather.

NAME ____________________ DATE __________

Problem Solving

Directions: Use page 58 to answer these questions. First, skim the paragraphs to find information that might help you solve the problem. Remember to show your thinking as you do the math!

1. How many pounds of material does it take to make one batch of concrete? ________

   Write a fraction to show what part of the mixture is cement. ________

   Write a fraction to show what part of the mixture is sand. ________

   Write a fraction to show what part of the mixture is crushed rock or gravel. ________

   Write a fraction to show what part of the mixture is water. ________

2. Try cutting the amounts of each material in half.

   What is the total weight of one batch in pounds? ________

   How much cement would you need? ________

   Write a fraction to show what part of this mixture is cement. ________

   How much sand would you need? ________

   Write a fraction to show what part of this mixture is sand. ________

   How much crushed rock or gravel would you need? ________

   Write a fraction to show what part of this mixture is rock or gravel. ________

   How much water would you need? ________

   Write a fraction to show what part of this mixture is water. ________

NAME ______________________________ DATE ______________

Engage

Directions: You can explore math in the real world. Discuss how the math in the passage on page 58 applies to other things you see in life.

1. The commutative property means it doesn't matter the order in which things happen. Which part of making cement follows this rule?

   ____

   Which part of making cement does not follow the commutative property?

   ____

2. Which part of making concrete follows the commutative property?

   ____

   Which part of making concrete does not follow this rule? ______________________________

   ____

3. Which math operations follow this property? ______________________________

   Which math operations do not follow this property? ______________________________

4. What are other ways you have seen the commutative property at work?

   ____

   ____

   What are some times when the commutative property does not work?

   ____

   ____

5. What is the most interesting thing you learned about concrete?

   ____

   ____

   What are some helpful ways people use concrete?

   ____

   ____

NAME ______________________________ DATE ______________

A Five-Hundred-Year-Old Snack

The food known as *quesadillas* dates back hundreds of years. In its simplest form, it is a tortilla folded over a simple filling and fried. When the Spanish people arrived in Central America, the natives had already perfected making tortillas. This flat bread was made from ground corn, or maize.

Cheese was found in both the Old World and the New World. It is a common filling for a quesadilla. The name means "little cheesy thing" in Spanish. The type of cheese used is a mild white cheese, similar to Monterey Jack. Regions in the south add variety to the quesadilla. In some areas of Mexico, the tortilla is folded over herbs and peppers. Other people fold it over potatoes and chorizo, a type of sausage.

The Spanish people brought their own ideas for fillings. They introduced chicken as a filling. They also used beef, seafood, or vegetables. Natives included squash blossoms or corn blossoms. These were best during the rainy months.

If the cheese is placed between two tortillas and then all fried at once, it is called a *sincronizada*. Sometimes meat is added with the cheese in this dish.

No matter how you slice it, a quesadilla makes a tasty snack!

THINK ABOUT THE MATH

- Equivalent fractions represent the same part of a whole.
- Whole numbers can be expressed as fractions: $3 = \frac{3}{1}$
- Compare the numerators and denominators of fractions to determine which fraction describes a larger share.
- Shapes can be divided into parts with equal areas.
- The area of each part of a shape is a fraction of the whole.
- Use a visual model to determine if two fractions are equal.
- Compare fractions that are part of the same whole.
- Use a fraction to describe part of a shape.

NAME ______________________ DATE __________

Problem Solving

Directions: Use page 61 to answer these questions. First, skim the paragraphs to find information that might help you solve the problem. Remember to show your thinking as you do the math!

1. If two friends share a quesadilla, how much of the tortilla will each person have? Write equivalent fractions to express your answer.

   Draw a picture of a quesadilla divided into two equal shares.

2. What shape does each portion look like? Explain your answer.

   ____

   ____

3. How many tortillas would it take to feed 6 people if each person had one half of a quesadilla? ______________

4. Two tortillas are stacked with cheese in the middle to make the dish that is similar to a quesadilla. If the *sincronizada* is cut into quarters, how many people can share the snack?

   ____

   Draw a picture to show how to cut the *sincronizada*.

NAME ______________________________ DATE ______________

Engage

Directions: Think about the food you read about in the reading passage on page 61. Answer the questions below. Then, discuss your answers with classmates.

1. What are the main ingredients of a quesadilla? ______________________________

   Why is this food called a quesadilla? ______________________________

   ____

2. Who probably first made quesadillas? ______________________________

   ____

3. What are some other ingredients that can be included?

   ____

   ____

   ____

4. What food have you had that is most similar to a quesadilla?

   ____

5. Describe a time when you have had a quesadilla. If you have not had it, describe the way you think you would like it best and when you might like to eat it.

   ____

   ____

   ____

   ____

   ____

   ____

   ____

   ____

   ____

   ____

NAME ______________________ DATE ____________

Making Trail Mix

THINK ABOUT THE MATH

- Equivalent fractions represent the same part of a whole.
- Compare the numerators and denominators of fractions to determine which fraction describes a larger share.
- A picture graph uses pictures or symbols to show information about groups of objects.
- A bar graph is a chart that uses rectangular bars to compare information.
- Use a visual fraction model to determine if two fractions are equal.
- Compare fractions that are part of the same whole.
- Include a key on a picture graph to show what the symbols on the graph mean.
- Number the scale on a bar graph to show how many objects each category might have.

Kiara put her pencil and papers in her desk. She smoothed out the paper towel the class helper had given her. Today they would measure the ingredients for trail mix and make graphs. That part would be fun. Even better would be their science walk that afternoon. They would take their snacks on the trail.

"I hope Mrs. Mitchell doesn't add peanuts. Luis can't have peanuts," she said to Dylan, who sat next to Kiara.

"It will be fine. Mrs. Mitchell always thinks about what everyone can have."

Mrs. Mitchell showed the class a set of measuring cups. She wrote the name of each cup on the board. "The other third-grade class will go on the hike with us. We'll need to make a double batch of trail mix." She wrote the amount of each food needed for the recipe. "Think about how much of each ingredient we will need for a double batch and write it on your paper."

Kiara copied the ingredient words on her graph. She made a list of the ingredient amounts. Then she tried to figure how much of each it would take for a double batch. Kiara watched as their teacher called students to measure foods and add them to a huge metal bowl.

It didn't look to Kiara as if there would be enough of each ingredient in the small snack cups to make much of a graph. Maybe she and Dylan could combine their portions to make their graphs more interesting. She glanced sideways at him. After they made their graphs, they could separate the trail mix again.

Dylan raised his hand. "Um, shouldn't there be more chocolate?" he asked when the teacher called on him.

"This is a snack, not dessert," Mrs. Mitchell smiled. "One person from each table may come and get a tray of cups for your table." She poured the trail mix into snack cups. Then she put the remaining trail mix in a large bag for the other class to divide.

NAME ______________________ DATE ____________

Problem Solving

Directions: Use page 64 to answer these questions. First, skim the paragraphs to find information that might help you solve the problem. Remember to show your thinking as you do the math!

1. Write the amount of each ingredient needed to make a double batch.

$1\frac{1}{2}$ cups almonds	________
$1\frac{1}{2}$ cups cashews	________
$\frac{3}{4}$ cup dried banana chips	________
1 cup dried cranberries	________
$\frac{1}{3}$ cup dark chocolate chips	________
$1\frac{1}{2}$ cups multi-grain cereal	________

2. Which ingredients in the recipe are added in equivalent amounts?

____

____

3. How many times will Kiara fill a $\frac{1}{2}$ cup to measure the cereal for one batch? ________

How many times will she fill a $\frac{1}{2}$ cup to measure cereal for a double batch? ________

Draw visual models to show the number of half cups needed.

4. How many times will Dylan fill a $\frac{1}{3}$ cup with chocolate chips to make a double batch?

____

5. Does the recipe have more dark chocolate chips or more banana chips? Draw a visual model to show how you know.

NAME ____________________ DATE ____________

Engage **Directions:** Complete the tasks below.

cashews

almonds

dark chocolate chips

dried cranberries

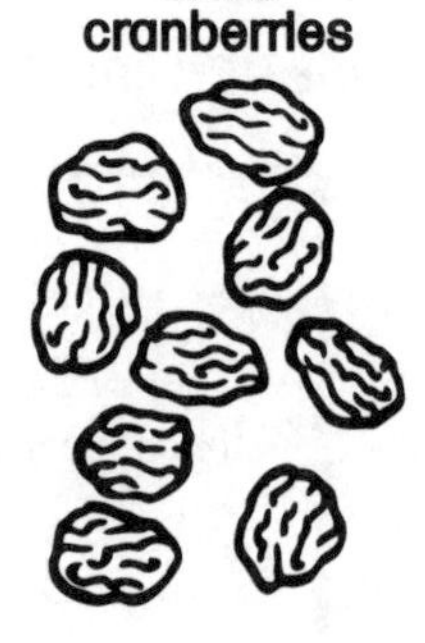

dried banana chips

1. Refer to the picture to create a picture graph that displays how many of each ingredient Kiara had in her cup of trail mix.

2. How many objects does one picture on your graph represent? Explain why you chose this for the key on your graph.

____

____

____

Key

3. Dylan has twice as many almonds and half as many dark chocolate chips as Kiara. He decides to use the data from his cup of trail mix to make a bar graph. Draw a bar graph to show the number of items in each ingredient category on Dylan's graph.

4. What number scale did you use for the graph? Why?

____

____

____

NAME ______________________________ DATE __________

A Red Moon

About once a month we see a full moon. The part of the moon that reflects light from the sun is actually half of the moon. It looks like a full circle. We call this a full moon. When there is a full moon, Earth and the moon and sun line up.

Sometimes there is a lunar eclipse. This happens when Earth's shadow blocks the sun's light. It happens when there is a full moon. In a total eclipse, all of Earth's shadow covers the moon. It usually takes about two hours for the moon to pass into and back out of Earth's shadow. Some light from the sun is reflected even when a shadow completely covers the moon. We still see the moon, but it is very dim.

The light that reflects best is red. During the total part of a lunar eclipse, the moon looks red. It is like having all Earth's sunrises and sunsets reflected back on the moon.

There was a total lunar eclipse on April 4, 2015. The moon was completely in Earth's shadow for about 5 minutes. The whole eclipse lasted for 3 hours and 29 minutes. Another one happened on September 28, 2015. These were the third and fourth in a series of four such events.

Each place on Earth can see a lunar eclipse every two and a half years.

The next total eclipse will be on January 31, 2018. The total eclipse will last one hour and 16 minutes. The eclipse in September 2015 was for a total of one hour and 12 minutes.

THINK ABOUT THE MATH

- There are 60 minutes in an hour.
- A number line diagram can be used to figure time in hours and minutes.
- Estimation and rounding strategies can help you figure the number of days, weeks, or months between events.
- Draw a number line to show hours and minutes.
- Count the number of days in a month.
- Diagrams can help us understand what we read in science and math.

NAME ________________________ DATE __________

Problem Solving

Directions: Use page 67 to answer these questions. First, skim the paragraphs to find information that might help you solve the problem. Remember to show your thinking as you do the math!

1. About how many minutes does it take for the moon to pass into and back out of Earth's shadow? ______________

2. How many minutes did the April 2015 eclipse last? ______________

   Draw a number line diagram to show how you found your answer.

   How much of that was a total eclipse? ______________

   For how much time was the eclipse not a total eclipse? Express the time in hours and minutes. ______________

3. How many days were there between the third and fourth total lunar eclipses in 2015? ______________

   Explain how you found your answer. ______________

   ____

4. How many minutes will the total part of the 2018 eclipse last? ______________

   How many minutes did the total part of the September 2015 eclipse last? ______________

   In which year will the total eclipse part last longer? ______________

   How much longer? ______________

   Use a number line diagram to help you find the length of each eclipse.

   What kind of visual model besides a number line diagram could you use to find the length of each eclipse? ______________

NAME ______________________ DATE __________

Engage **Directions:** Use the information from the passage and other resources to answer the questions below.

1. What is a lunar eclipse? ______________________

____

Draw a diagram to show your understanding of a lunar eclipse based on what you have read.

2. What causes a red moon? ______________________

____

____

3. How is a lunar eclipse different from a solar eclipse? ______________________

____

4. When will the next lunar eclipse happen (after January 2018)? ______________________

5. If possible, use a time and date calculator on the Internet to learn the next time (after January 2018) an eclipse (solar or lunar) will be visible in your town. Write a paragraph telling people in your community about this event.

____

____

____

____

____

NAME ______________________ DATE ____________

Worth the Wait

THINK ABOUT THE MATH

- There are 60 minutes in one hour.
- Place value helps us round numbers.
- Multiplication and division are used to solve word problems involving equal groups.
- Use a number line to add or subtract time in minutes.
- Round minutes to the nearest 30 or 60 to estimate times.

Ty patted the seat next to him as he urged Micah to hurry into the shuttle. He didn't want to miss a minute of their day at Disneyland.

"What ride shall we go on first?" Mom leaned across the aisle of the van.

"Space Mountain!" Micah's look showed he had definite ideas about the order in which they would do things.

Ty shook his head. "No, Splash Mountain."

Mom grinned. "We'll save that one for the afternoon, when it's hot."

"The one with the shortest line," Dad said. Ty wished he were close enough to give Dad a playful punch in the arm.

Once they got in the park, Mom suggested they make a list of the rides. Each person could put a star next to the ride he wanted to go on the most. They would do those 4 rides today and see how much time they had left. Mom said they would think about the lines at each ride and the weather, too.

They started at Space Mountain because Dad said the lines would get too long later in the day. Ty and Micah instantly declared it their favorite ride of all time. Next, Mom wanted to go to Big Thunder Mountain Railroad before it got hot. Ty went along to please Mom, but it was so tame compared to Space Mountain!

After lunch they enjoyed the activities along the way as they waited for Indiana Jones. The line at Astro Blasters was longer than Indiana Jones, but still not too long. By this time it was late in the afternoon, and they were ready to cool down.

"Time for Splash Mountain!" Ty cheered. What a long wait, but it was worth it!

NAME ______________________________ DATE ____________

Problem Solving

Directions: Use page 70 to answer these questions. First, skim the paragraphs to find information that might help you solve the problem. Remember to show your thinking as you do the math!

1. Ty's family entered the park at 9:00 a.m. It took about 20 minutes to get organized. They waited 28 minutes in line at Space Mountain. The ride lasted 2 minutes. What time did they get done at Space Mountain? ______________________

   If they had waited until later in the day to ride Space Mountain, the wait would have been 58 minutes.

   How much less time did Ty and Micah wait in line by going earlier in the day? ________

2. Before lunch, the family went on Big Thunder Mountain Railroad. They waited 27 minutes in line. After lunch, they waited in line for Indiana Jones. The wait was 39 minutes, but they enjoyed the activities along the way.

   For which ride did they wait the longest? ______________________

   How much longer did they wait? ______________________

   Which wait was the closest to a half-hour wait? ______________________

3. Round the wait times in question 2 to the nearest 10 to estimate the total amount of time Ty waited for the two rides.

   ____

   Based on your answer, would you say he waited less than an hour or more than an hour for those two rides?

   ____

   Check your estimate by adding the exact times Ty waited for each ride.

   ____

4. The wait for Splash Mountain was 69 minutes. How many hours and how many minutes did Ty wait?

   ____

5. How much total time did the boys spend waiting in line to go on the 4 rides the family chose? ______________________

   To the nearest hour, about how long did they wait in line? ______________

NAME ____________________ DATE __________

Engage

Directions: Think about the number of people who wait in line for rides. Use groups of people (such as a family), wait times, amount of distance needed for people standing in line, or ticket costs to write questions for classmates about an amusement park.

NAME ______________________________ DATE ____________

Summer Eating Fun

We often think of watermelon as a summertime food. Different kinds of watermelon grow in different places. Farmers have new ways to ship produce. It is possible to have watermelon year-round.

This healthy fruit has high water content. That means most of its weight is water. About three-quarters of a watermelon is fruit. A little over one quarter is rind. Did you know the whole watermelon is okay to eat?

An average watermelon in the store weighs 20 pounds.

China grows more watermelon than any other country. Watermelon first grew wild in Africa. It likes warmer temperatures. In the United States, it grows in California and Georgia. It also grows in Florida and Texas.

At home, watermelon will keep for 7 to 10 days at room temperature. Wrap cut watermelon and store it in the refrigerator.

It is easy to choose a good watermelon when you shop. Look for a firm melon. It should not have cuts, bruises, or dents. It should be heavy for its size. There will be a creamy yellow spot on one side where it sat on the ground and ripened in the sun. Take the watermelon home. Cut it into wedges or cubes and enjoy!

THINK ABOUT THE MATH

- Grams (g) are the standard unit of measurement of mass or weight.
- 1 kilogram (kg) is equal to 1,000 g.
- One pound weighs the same as about 500 g.
- A fraction shows the number of equal parts in a whole.
- Use place-value strategies to multiply multiples of 10.
- Use a letter to stand for an unknown number in an equation.
- Find the number of parts in the numerator of a fraction to mark off a line segment on a number line.

NAME ______________________ DATE __________

Problem Solving

Directions: Use page 73 to answer these questions. First, skim the paragraphs to find information that might help you solve the problem. Remember to show your thinking as you do the math!

1. About how many grams (g) does an average watermelon weigh? __________

2. How many kilograms (kg) does a 9,000 g watermelon weigh? __________

3. Some watermelons are "personal" watermelons. They are smaller and have a thinner rind. These melons weigh about 3,000 g each. How many kg does one personal watermelon weigh?

   ____

4. How many more grams does an average watermelon weigh than a personal watermelon?

   ____

5. One of the heaviest watermelons was grown in 2005 in Arkansas. It weighed 268 pounds. Another way to measure its mass is to say it weighed about 134 kg.

   How much heavier was this watermelon than a 20-pound watermelon in a store (in pounds)?

   ____

   How many more kg did this watermelon weigh than an average 9 kg watermelon?

   ____

NAME ______________________ DATE __________

Engage

Directions: Think about how many people one watermelon will feed. Then, answer the questions below.

1. How much of a watermelon is fruit? ______________________

   Draw a watermelon and shade a fraction to show how much is fruit.

   How many equal parts did you divide your drawing into? ______________

2. Draw a number line. Number it 1 to 20 and divide it into 4 equal parts. Draw a line segment to show how much of the watermelon is fruit.

   How many pounds of fruit are in a 20-pound watermelon? ______________

3. A group that promotes watermelon says there are about 3 cups of fruit for every pound of watermelon.

   How many cups of fruit are in an average watermelon? ______________________

   Explain how you found your answer. ______________________

   ____

4. If one serving of watermelon equals 1 cup of diced fruit, how many servings are in one average watermelon? ______________

5. How many cups of watermelon might one person eat? ______________

   How does the amount each person eats change the number of people who might be able to share a watermelon?

   ____

NAME ______________________ DATE __________

Antoine Lavoisier: Chemistry for Everyone

THINK ABOUT THE MATH

- We use grams to measure the mass of an object.
- There are 1,000 g in 1 kg.
- Liquid volume describes how much liquid a container can hold.
- There are 1,000 mL in 1 liter.
- There are 10 groups of 10 in 100.
- Division is an unknown factor problem.
- Draw a picture to show what is happening in a measurement problem.
- Find the number of parts in the numerator of a fraction to mark off a line segment on a number line.
- Use multiplication to solve division problems.

Scientists study the nature of things. They work to learn more about our world. Antoine Lavoisier lived in France over two hundred years ago. People call him the father of modern chemistry. His family had enough money that he was able to get a good education.

Paris had a problem providing enough clean water for people in a large city. Antoine mapped the main water supply in Paris by the time he was 25 years old. He was granted a membership in the Royal Academy of Sciences.

Antoine worked with salts, bases, and acids. He also worked with oxygen. He developed a list of elements. The list later became today's periodic table of elements. He discovered that water is a compound made up of two elements. A molecule of water has two hydrogen atoms and one oxygen atom. Some of his most famous experiments were with combustion, or burning. He proved that oxygen plays a role in this process.

Scientists measure mass in grams and volume in liters. Often, experiments combine substances to observe chemical reactions. The capacity of a liquid is measured in liters. Other units of measurement are also used. Antoine measured carefully in his experiments. His methods led to the creation of the metric system. Other scientists started using scientific methods in their own research.

NAME ______________________ DATE __________

Problem Solving

Directions: Use page 76 to answer these questions. First, skim the paragraphs to find information that might help you solve the problem. Remember to show your thinking as you do the math!

1. There are 1,000 g in 1 liter of water. What is another way to describe the mass of 1 liter of water?

   ____

   How much mass does 2 liters of water have? ______________________

2. People need water to survive. Our bodies are about 60% water. This is the same as 60 parts out of 100.

   How many parts out of 10 would this be? ______________________

   Draw a number line and mark it in increments of ten.

   Draw a line segment to show how much of our bodies are water.

3. Some people say that the human body needs 2,200 mL of fluid per day. Other people say that our bodies need eight 8 oz. glasses of liquid per day, which is about 2,000 mL. What is the difference in the amount of liquid suggested by these two different sources?

   ____

4. All fluids count toward the total amount of liquid a person might drink in one day. However, water has no calories and is inexpensive. If you had 200 mL of juice at breakfast and 250 mL of milk at dinner, how much water should you have during the rest of the day if you're following the first advice given in the question above?

   ____

NAME ______________________ DATE __________

Engage

Directions: Research and find a science experiment involving capacity you would like to try. Use milliliters and liters to measure the liquids in your experiment. Measure carefully and record your observations and results of the experiment.

1. Ask a question. What would you like to learn about how liquids interact?

2. List the liquids you will work with in your experiment.

3. How much of each liquid do you think you will need?

4. What will you change if you do not get the results you expect?

5. Describe what happened when you did your experiment. Add drawings to your explanation and share your results with classmates.

   For example, what happens if you add soda and vinegar to water? How much vinegar do you need to obtain an observable result? How much water do you need?

   How much food coloring does it take to turn water a desired color? How much water is the best amount to use?

NAME ______________________ DATE ____________

Recycling by the Numbers

We read and hear a lot about recycling. We know it's good for the environment. Programs in our cities and towns make it easier to recycle now than in years past. It is possible to recycle paper, glass, and many plastics. Homes have marked bins to help people remember to recycle these things. In some places, people do not have to sort what they recycle; it all goes in one bin. In other towns, people separate the glass, paper, and plastic. Some places recycle metal, too.

Different groups keep track of how much people recycle. They try to help people learn how to recycle. They list the amounts of different materials that people recycle.

Most paper mills use recycled paper. They use recycled materials to make new paper. Many systems can remove staples. People might want to take paper clips off paper, though, and use them again. More cardboard is recycled than paper.

Glass can be reused many times and still hold its strength. Most glass that people recycle consists of food and drink containers.

Plastic comes in different types. On the bottom of many plastic containers is a number inside a triangle. This is a symbol that tells the type of plastic in the item. A few places have people sort plastics at home, but most plastics are sorted at a facility.

Things that are recycled do not go to the landfill. This helps our environment.

THINK ABOUT THE MATH

- A picture graph uses pictures or symbols to show information about groups of objects.
- A bar graph is a chart that uses rectangular bars to compare information.
- The key on a picture graph tells how many objects each symbol stands for.
- The scale on a bar graph shows how many of each object are in each category.
- A category is a group of things that have something in common.
- Draw a picture graph to show how many objects are in each category.
- Decide how many objects each single picture will represent.
- Include a key on a picture graph to show what the symbols on the graph mean.
- Number the scale on a bar graph to show how many objects each category might have.

NAME ____________________ DATE __________

Problem Solving

Directions: Use page 79 to answer these questions. First, skim the paragraphs to find information that might help you solve the problem. Remember to show your thinking as you do the math!

- 63 pieces of paper out of every 100 are recycled.
- 9 pieces of plastic out of every 100 pieces are recycled.
- 14 plastic bags out of every 100 are recycled.
- 27 glass items are recycled out of every 100.
- 55 pieces of aluminum are recycled out of every 100.

1. Use the list above to create a picture graph on the back of this page.

   What symbol(s) will you use for each category? ____________________

   How many objects will each single symbol represent? ____________________

   What categories will you list across the bottom of your graph? ____________________

   ____

2. Which category has the most recycled items? ____________________

   Which category has the least amount of recycled items? ____________________

3. What is the difference between the amount of glass and the amount of aluminum recycled? ____________________

4. If a waste-collection truck recycles 270 glass items at the end of its run, how many glass objects in the community were collected? __________ Refer to the list above to find the relationship between recycled items and those that are not recycled. Then work through this problem with the questions below.

   What is the relationship between 27 and 270? ____________________

   How can you apply this to the total amount of glass? ____________________

   Use place-value strategies, multiples of 10, and properties of multiplication to think about how to find the number of glass objects not recycled.

5. What reasons can you think of to explain the results listed above? Think about which category has the most recycled items and which category has the least.

   ____

   ____

NAME ______________________________ DATE ____________

Engage **Directions:** Use the information in the list on page 80 to make a bar graph.

1. What equal parts make the most sense for your scale on the left side of the graph?

____

Where will your numbering start and end?

____

2. How does your completed graph compare with the picture graph you drew for question 1 on page 80?

____

How are the graphs similar? ______________________________

How are they different? ______________________________

3. Looking at the bar graph, how would you describe the difference between the two plastic categories and the two other container (glass and metal) categories?

____

Write and solve an equation to find the difference between the amount of glass and the amount of paper recycled.

Write a true number sentence using >, <, or = to compare the amount of glass recycled to the amount of paper.

4. Looking at the bar graph, which two categories are most similar in amount of items recycled? ______________________________

Which two categories have the greatest difference? ______________________________

5. Use the information from the list and your graphs to write one new question for classmates.

____

____

NAME ______________________________ DATE ____________

Croaks Around the World

THINK ABOUT THE MATH

- A number line may be marked off in $\frac{1}{4}$- and $\frac{1}{2}$-inch increments to represent a ruler.
- On a line plot, each data value is shown as an X or a dot above a number line.

- Use a ruler to measure lengths in inches.
- Use a number line as a visual model to find differences in length of objects, measured in inches.
- Use a line plot to compare lengths of objects.

Frogs live on every continent except Antarctica. Countries in the tropics have a greater variety of frogs. Costa Rica lies between the Atlantic and Pacific Oceans. It is close to where North and South America meet. Over 125 species of frogs and toads live in its warm tropical climate.

We may not think of frogs as very colorful animals. Many are green or brown, the color of their surroundings. Poison dart frogs do not blend in with their environment. Their bright colors warn predators to stay away. The amount of poison in their skin depends on their diet.

The most colorful type of frog in Costa Rica is the blue jeans poison dart frog. They are bright red with blue markings on their legs. Some are bright red with black spots and do not have the blue markings. These are called strawberry dart frogs. Some have green markings on their legs.

These tiny frogs grow to be $\frac{3}{4}$ to 1 inch long. Other poison dart frogs are not as small. The golden dart frog is twice the size—up to 2 inches in length. It has enough venom to kill 10 people.

Equally colorful, but not poisonous, the red-eyed tree frog lives in similar habitats. It uses bright coloring to scare predators away. The frog suddenly shows bright red eyes and orange webbed feet when disturbed by predators. It can be $1\frac{1}{2}$ inches to $2\frac{3}{4}$ inches in length.

Many other kinds of frogs live around the world. They vary in size, with some reaching 6 inches in length. The largest frog discovered is about 12 inches long! It comes as no surprise that this huge frog has the name Goliath frog. It lives in West Africa at the equator.

On a summer night, you might hear frogs. Their croaks remind us that children in other places hear frogs, too.

NAME ______________________ DATE __________

Problem Solving

Directions: Use page 82 to answer these questions. First, skim the paragraphs to find information that might help you solve the problem. Remember to show your thinking as you do the math!

1. Draw a number line and mark it like a ruler with $\frac{1}{4}$-inch increments. Start at 0 and number it to 3 (inches).

   How many equal parts are between 0 and 1? ______________________

   How many equal parts are between 2 and 3? ______________________

Use the reading passage and the number line above to answer the next four questions.

2. The smallest poison dart frog is between ________ inch and ________ inch.

   What's the difference in size? ______________________

3. What is the difference in size between a golden dart frog and the smallest poison dart frog?

   ____

4. How much larger is a small red-eyed tree frog than a large poison dart frog (*Note:* not the golden dart frog)?

   ____

5. What is the range in the size of red-eyed tree frogs?

   ____

NAME ______________________ DATE __________

Engage **Directions:** Use what you know about rulers to create a line plot to compare the different sizes of frogs.

1. Draw a line plot and mark off the scale in $\frac{1}{4}$, $\frac{1}{2}$, and whole-inch increments from 0 to 3. Plot the different sizes of frogs (under 3 inches) described in the reading passage on the line plot.

2. African dwarf frogs grow up to $1\frac{1}{2}$ inches. Add this frog to the line plot you started in question 1.

   Females might grow up to $\frac{1}{2}$ inch larger. What might be the total size of a female African dwarf frog? ______________________

   Add this to the line plot.

3. Coqui frogs live in Puerto Rico. These small frogs range in size from $1\frac{1}{4}$ inches (male) to $1\frac{1}{2}$ inches (female). Add these frogs on the line plot.

4. The American green tree frog is common in the United States. In the wild, they grow to about 2 inches. Their croak can be heard up to a mile away. Add this species to the line plot.

5. Measure the fingers on your hand. Write down the measurements in inches.

   index finger __________ ring finger __________

   middle finger __________ little finger __________

   Which frogs most closely match which fingers?

   ____

   ____

   ____

   ____

NAME ______________________________ DATE ____________

Shelter from a Storm

"Ryan!" Mom called. "Tornado warning! Please take this water and food and go to the storm shelter."

With a sigh, Ryan slung his backpack over his shoulders. He never knew how long they would be down there. His library book, along with some other things, would give him something to do. Mom didn't argue about the backpack, as long as he kept his hands free to carry whatever she needed.

"This is the third watch this week," he said, as Mom handed him two cloth tote bags. "Are you sure we need to go?"

"Yes." Mom's voice was firm. "We'd rather be safe than sorry."

She was right, Ryan knew. They got news magazines in reading class at school. Sometimes they read a story about damage from a severe storm. They had also read about times in history when people needed to take shelter from other threats. The threats could be war or nuclear stuff. At least with a storm there weren't any people causing the bad things. Weather was just one of those things that happened.

"Will you play a game with me?" Ryan's sister begged once they were in the small room. The cramped space was never intended for them to spend extended amounts of time. It was made of strong materials designed to withstand very high wind speeds. They kept battery-powered lights and blankets in the room. They also had an emergency radio and other supplies.

It would be more peaceful and pleasant if the time passed quickly, so Ryan agreed. He kept one of his favorite games in his pack. He took out the folded cardboard playing board and a small container of playing pieces. He set up the count-and-capture game and reminded Sarah how to play.

THINK ABOUT THE MATH

- We find the area of a rectangle by multiplying the length by the width.
- Figures can be decomposed into smaller rectangles.
- The perimeter of a figure is the distance around its outside edge.
- We find the perimeter of a figure by adding all of the side lengths.
- Use a model to show that the area of a rectangle is equal to multiplying the length by the width.
- Use the distributive property to find the area of rectangles when needed.
- Decompose figures into non-overlapping rectangles.
- Add areas of multiple smaller rectangles to find the area of the larger figure.

NAME ______________________ DATE ____________

Problem Solving

Directions: Use page 85 to answer these questions. First, skim the paragraphs to find information that might help you solve the problem. Remember to show your thinking as you do the math!

1. Ryan's family has a storm shelter that is 48 sq. ft. Draw and label a picture to show the possible length and width.

2. What is the perimeter of the shelter you designed in question 1? ____________

   What is the area of the shelter? ____________

   Write an equation to show how your measurements equal the area of the space.

3. What other length and width measurements could the shelter have and still have the same area? Draw and label a picture.

   What is the perimeter of this shelter? ____________ How is it the same or different from the perimeter of the first shelter?

   ____

4. There are four people in Ryan's family. How many sq. ft. does each person have in the storm shelter? ____________

5. Guidelines suggest that each person have at least 7 square feet for a hurricane- and tornado-safe shelter.
   What would be the area of such a shelter for Ryan's family? ____________

   How much larger is his family's shelter? ____________

6. Why do you think storm shelters might be based on square feet per person instead of perimeter? ______________________________

   ____

NAME ______________________ DATE __________

Engage **Directions:** Model a storm shelter in your classroom by measuring a space and marking it with tape or string. Then, answer the questions below.

1. Work in groups of 4 to mark out a shelter space that would give each person in your group at least 7 square feet. Should a storm shelter allow more or less space per person? __________

2. What is the length and width of the shelter space your group designed in the classroom? __________

   What is the perimeter? __________

3. What other lengths and widths did other groups use to create their shelters? Make a list to show combinations.

length	width	perimeter	square feet	square feet per person

   What do you notice about how perimeter relates to square feet? __________

   ____

4. If every group had their storm shelters combined into one large shelter, what would the total area be?

   ____

5. What type of storm shelter might be most appropriate in your area? Research to learn about types of storms or other natural disasters. Share the types of things people do to stay safe from these events in your town.

   ____

   ____

   ____

NAME ______________________________ DATE ____________

Let's Play Ball!

THINK ABOUT THE MATH

- A quadrilateral is a closed figure with four sides and four angles.
- An angle is a figure formed by two lines that start at the same point.
- Two parallel lines stay the same distance from each other and never cross.
- A parallelogram is a quadrilateral with opposite sides that are equal in length and parallel.
- A rectangle is a parallelogram with four right angles.
- A rhombus is a quadrilateral with four sides that are the same length.
- Opposite angles of a rhombus are the same.
- The difference between a rectangle and a rhombus is that the angles of a rhombus are not always right angles.
- A square is a special type of parallelogram. It has four right angles. It has four sides that are the same length.
- Use a ruler to draw straight lines.
- Use a tile or corner of a piece of paper to draw right angles.
- Use the attributes of shapes to identify and name them.

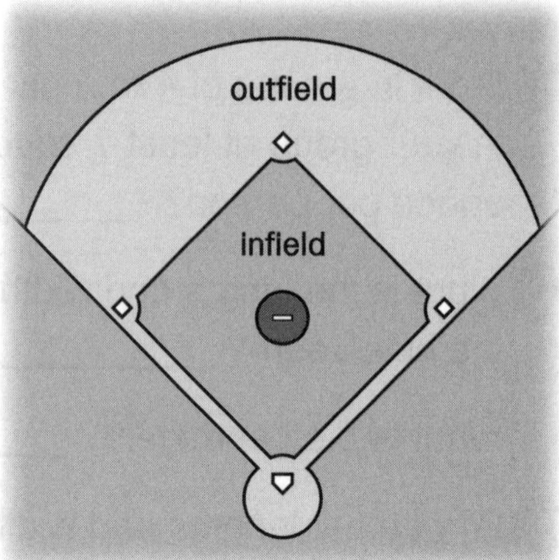

The game of baseball is as old as the United States. Colonists played a game that combined parts of two different games from England. Some people in New York formed a club. They played a game they called baseball. One of the people in the club made a new set of rules. The rules made the game different than the games from England. He said the infield would be a certain shape with foul lines. There were three bases and home plate. Players were allowed three strikes. The fielding team could not throw balls at the runners to tag them out. These changes made the game safer and faster paced.

Players learned through trial and error the best length between bases. The length between each base is 90 feet. This is just enough space to allow the runner to reach a base without being caught too often. It is not too far apart for fielders to throw the ball between bases.

The distance between the pitcher's plate and home plate is carefully measured. It has been the same since 1893. There are many rules about the height and size of the pitcher's mound. The pitcher stands on a rubber plate in the center of the mound.

Foul lines show when a ball is fair or out of bounds. Poles next to the fence at the edge of the outfield help an umpire tell if a home run is a fair ball. Fans cheer for their teams, especially when home runs are hit!

NAME ______________________ DATE ____________

Problem Solving

Directions: Use page 88 to answer these questions. First, skim the paragraphs to find information that might help you solve the problem. Remember to show your thinking as you do the math!

1. What shape is the baseball infield in the diagram on page 88? ____________

   What characteristics does it have that define it as that shape? ____________

   ____

2. First, second, and third base are marked by a bag filled with soft material. The bag has four sides. Each side is 15 inches.

   What shape is the bag? ____________

   How do you know? ____________

3. Home plate has one edge that is 17 inches long. The sides next to this big side are $8\frac{1}{2}$ inches long. The last two sides form a point. They are 12 inches long. Use cm as a standard measurement length to draw a picture of home plate on the back of this page. What shape did you draw? ____________

   Why do you think it is this shape for this sport? ____________

   ____

4. The pitcher's mound has a diameter of 18 ft. Draw the pitcher's mound. Label the diameter.

   What shape did you draw? ____________

5. The pitcher's plate is 24 inches long and 6 inches wide. Draw a picture and label the sides.

   What shape is it? ____________

   What characteristics define this shape?

   ____

   ____

NAME ______________________ DATE ____________

Engage **Directions:** Use what you have learned about shapes to make a model of a baseball field. Then, answer the questions below.

1. Use tape, string, or yarn to mark out a baseball field in the classroom. Baseball fields have measurements in feet.

   Which standard measurement unit could you use to best mark a baseball field that fits in the classroom? ____________

2. Which shape best describes your baseball field? ____________

   Explain your answer. ____________

3. How many inches are between each base? ____________

4. How would you define the point where the base lines meet at the base markers?

NAME ______________________________ DATE ____________

Think Outside the Box

How companies package their products makes a difference in how well they sell. Many things are on the same store shelf. Each company wants people to notice its brand and buy its product.

Companies research and learn what catches shoppers' attention. They study what sells best. One company says that sharp, pointed edges make people notice a package.

Most researchers agree that the package must have clear information. People want to know what they're buying. Bright colors capture kids' attention.

Many things come in some sort of box. Box shapes are easy to stack in trucks and on store shelves. Some toy packages have a trapezoid shape. The top of the package is not as wide as the bottom. They can hang on a peg from a wall display.

Think about what would make a product easy to open or use. A different shape might work well. Studies show that people often find smooth or round shapes more pleasing.

A wonderful product still has to be noticed by people in the stores. That's where creative packaging can make a difference!

THINK ABOUT THE MATH

- A rhombus has four straight sides of equal length but usually does not have right angles.
- A parallelogram is a quadrilateral with opposite sides that are equal in length and parallel.
- A rectangle is a parallelogram with four right angles.
- A right angle is the corner, like the corner of a square, where two perpendicular lines intersect.
- Perpendicular lines cross each other at a right angle.
- Use the attributes of shapes to identify and name them.
- Use a ruler to draw shapes with straight sides.
- Use the corner of a piece of paper or a tile to determine if an angle is a right angle.

NAME ______________________ DATE ____________

Problem Solving

Directions: Use page 91 to answer these questions. First, skim the paragraphs to find information that might help you solve the problem. Remember to show your thinking as you do the math!

1. Which shape(s) would be most practical for shipping and storage? ____________

____

2. Which shape(s) might people be more attracted to? ____________

____

3. Use a ruler to draw a rectangle-shaped package.

What is true about the sides of your rectangle? ____________

Draw diagonal lines across your rectangle from each corner to its opposite corner. Measure the lines. What do you notice? ____________

____

4. When might a rhombus be a useful product shape? ____________

____

Use a ruler to draw a rhombus.

5. What is true about the sides of a rhombus? ____________

____

When is a rhombus not a square? ____________

____

NAME ______________________________ DATE ______________

Engage **Directions:** Design a package for your favorite toy. Then, answer the questions below.

1. What shape is the toy? ______________________________

   Draw a picture of the object you will package.

   What shape package would be best for it? Why? ______________________________

   ____

2. How can you make your package different from other toys like this? ______________

   ____

   Draw pictures of other packages you have seen for toys like this.

3. What shape package would catch kids' attention? ______________________________

   Draw some ideas. Ask classmates which package they might like to buy.

4. What about your design did your classmates like? Why did it catch their attention?

   ____

   ____

   ____

NAME ______________________________ DATE ____________

Wrapping a Gift

"Mom, where's the present for Naomi's party?" Andrew carried wrapping paper and tape as he wandered through the kitchen.

Mom dried her hands on a towel and told him to look on the desk. "Do you want help?"

"Yes, I want to make sure it looks nice." He unrolled the wrapping paper and set the box in the center.

"The present looks like a rectangle to me." Mom looked at Andrew to see what he would do next.

Andrew grinned. "But it's not a rhombus because it has square corners."

Mom pointed to the wrapping paper. "The present isn't flat. How will you know if you have enough wrapping paper?"

Andrew picked up one edge of the paper and held it over a side of the box. "That's one side and where it sits on the paper is the second side." He flipped the box over a couple of times. "Three sides, four sides."

"What will you do about the ends?"

He scooted the box sideways on the paper and held up the edge of the paper. "This almost covers one end." He held up the other edge against the opposite end of the box. "I'll cut some of this extra off, but maybe I should draw a line first." Andrew held the ruler next to the pencil to draw a straight line. Then Mom handed him the scissors.

THINK ABOUT THE MATH

- A prism is a solid object with identical ends, flat faces, and the same cross section all along its length.
- We can divide shapes into parts with equal areas.
- The area of each equal part of a shape is a fraction of the whole.
- Find the area of a rectangle by multiplying the length by the width.
- Division is an unknown factor problem.
- Use a fraction to describe part of a shape.
- Use the distributive property to find the area of rectangles when needed.
- Decompose figures into non-overlapping rectangles.
- Decompose numbers by tens to multiply or divide larger numbers.

NAME ______________________ DATE __________

Problem Solving

Directions: Use page 94 to answer these questions. First, skim the paragraphs to find information that might help you solve the problem. Remember to show your thinking as you do the math!

1. The gift is in a box. What do we call this type of shape?

____

2. How many faces does the box have?

____

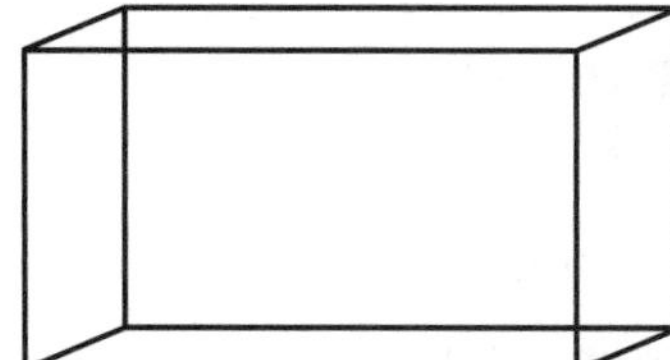

3. If all the faces have the same length and width, what shape is the box? __________

4. If a box has equal faces, how much of the total surface area is one face? __________

5. The ends of Andrew's box are not equal to the sides. The ends are 10" wide and 4" high. What is the area of one end of the box? __________

Label the drawing below to think about the area of the ends of the box.

NAME ______________________ DATE __________

Engage **Directions:** Work with classmates to figure out how much paper is needed to wrap a gift.

1. The top of Andrew's box was 16" long and 10" wide. What is the area of this side of the box?

   ____

   Draw a picture of the box if you can, or draw a picture of the top of the box to help you answer the question.

   What is the total area of the top and bottom sides of the box? ____________

2. The front of Andrew's box was 16" long and 4" wide. What is the area of this side of the box?

   ____

   What is the total area of the front and back sides of the box? ____________

3. The end of Andrew's box is 10" long and 4" wide. What is the total area of both ends of the box?

   ____

4. Andrew wants to cover the ends of the box using special wrapping paper. He has one piece of this special paper that is 7" long and 6" wide. What is the area of the special piece of wrapping paper that Andrew has?

   ____

   Does Andrew have enough of the special wrapping paper to cover the ends? ______

NAME ______________________ DATE __________

Setting Up to Play

Alex held the tape and started to pace around the blacktop area. "Let's mark out the squares."

"How big should they be?" Samantha asked. She liked to play foursquare, but the game wouldn't be as fun if they didn't get the squares right.

Waving a piece of paper, Carlos said, "I researched the official site. The boundaries of the main playing area are 16 feet on each side."

Alex's shoulders slumped. "It will take so long to set up, we won't have any time left to play."

"I'll get something to measure." Lauren jogged toward the school building.

"Once we have the court marked, we can use it more than once." Samantha bounced the ball and passed it to Alex.

He slid the roll of tape on his wrist and expertly caught the ball before it bounced away. "We'll lay out the whole playing area first," Alex planned. "Then we can divide the court."

"We divide it into equal parts," Carlos said consulting his paper. "Each person defends their area."

Lauren returned with a yardstick. "This is all I could find. Will it work?"

"Sure," Carlos said as he pointed to the side that had markings for inches and feet. "We'll just have to mark every three feet."

"Each side is supposed to be 16 feet," Samantha protested.

Carlos stuffed the paper in his pocket. Alex sent a bounce pass his direction, and he caught it and dribbled the ball. "It doesn't have to be that big. That's a lot of space for each person to defend."

"We'll see how much space we have when we actually start measuring." Alex took the yardstick from Lauren. "Didn't the rules suggest extra space for safety around the boundaries of the court?"

Nodding, Carlos held one end of the measuring stick for Alex. "Six feet," he agreed. "Do you have it marked so I can move my end of the yardstick?"

The bell rang, and Samantha groaned. They'd never get to play at this rate.

"Save your paper," Lauren laughed. "We'll need it again."

THINK ABOUT THE MATH

- We use multiplication to find the area of plane figures.
- The area of each equal part of a shape is a fraction of the whole.
- Use parentheses to show the order in which to do operations in an equation.
- Add areas of multiple smaller rectangles to find the area of a larger figure.
- Use a fraction to describe part of a shape.

NAME ____________________ DATE ____________

Problem Solving

Directions: Use page 97 to answer these questions. First, skim the paragraphs to find information that might help you solve the problem. Remember to show your thinking as you do the math!

1. What is the length of the sides of the whole playing area? ____________

   What shape do you think the court will be? ____________

   How do you know? ____________

   ____

2. How many people will play? ____________

   How many areas will they divide the court into for each person to have their own playing area? ____________

3. How many times will they need to lay the yardstick on the ground to measure the length of one side? ____________

4. Draw and label a picture of the playing court.

   How much of the total space will each person have? ____________

   Write this as a fraction. ____________

   What is the shape of each person's playing space? ____________

   What is the length of the sides of each person's playing area? ____________

5. What is the total playing area of the court? ____________

   Regroup by 10s and use properties of operations to find the total area. ____________

   What is the area of each person's playing space? ____________

   What is another way to find the area of the whole court? ____________

NAME ______________________________ DATE ____________

Engage **Directions:** Answer the following questions.

1. What is the perimeter of a standard foursquare court? ____________________

Refer to your drawing in question 4 on page 98.

Rewrite the perimeter as a multiplication problem.

2. If Alex allows 6 ft. on the outside edge all the way around as Carlos suggested, what is the total area they will need to set up their court? ____________________

____

3. Samantha decided 64 sq. ft. per player was too much space to defend, and Alex discovered they didn't have enough space on the blacktop to set up a court that large. They decided to have a court that gave each person 36 sq. ft. to defend. What was the size of each person's playing space? ____________

Draw and label their revised court.

4. If the court was divided as shown on the right, what would be the area of each player's section?

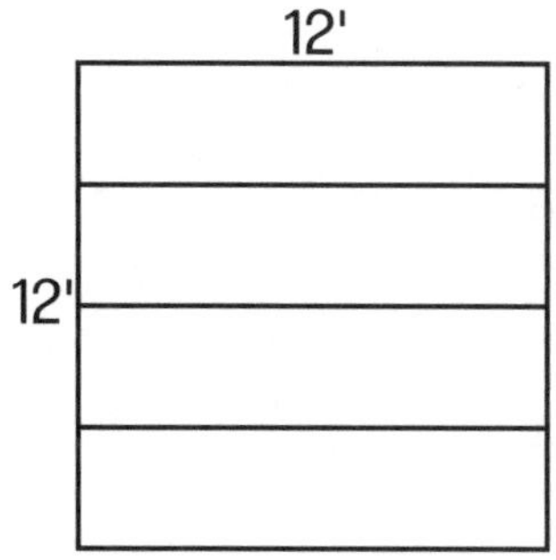

____

What would the total playing area be? ____________

Would the game still be called foursquare? ________

What could the new game be called? ____________________

NAME ______________________________ DATE ____________

Organizing a Closet

THINK ABOUT THE MATH

- We can divide shapes into parts with equal areas.
- The area of each part of a shape is a fraction of the whole.
- We measure area in square units.
- A fraction shows the number of equal parts in a whole.
- Draw pictures to visualize how an area can be divided into parts with equal areas.
- Use a fraction to describe part of a shape.
- Square units must not overlap or have gaps when measuring the area of a figure or space.

Mom came in with a stack of clothes. "We need to organize your closet."

Nevaeh groaned. It seemed to her that Mom's projects often resulted in a huge mess in her room that she had to clean up. "I have an idea," she said as she held up her hand to stop Mom before she got started. "Let's draw it out on paper so we know what we're trying to do."

"Good idea." Mom wiped her forehead from the warmth of the summer day. "I'll get lemonade, you get paper and pencil and a big eraser, and I'll meet you at the table."

Nevaeh almost couldn't keep from skipping as she got the supplies and went down the hall to the dining room. Disaster held off for another day. She might even have time to go outside and play in the sprinkler when they got done with the planning part.

"We could put a shelf in the closet." Nevaeh drew a rectangle on the paper, labeled it, and drew a line across the middle.

"That shouldn't be too difficult." Mom took a sip of lemonade. "How will that help you stay organized?"

Nevaeh drew a line near the top of the closet. Then she drew two evenly spaced vertical lines from the top of the closet to the shelf. "Brianna has cool dividers that hang from a closet rod. I could stack things on the shelf and they wouldn't fall over."

Mom nodded absently. "Let's think about this and come back to it tomorrow."

NAME ______________________________ DATE ____________

Problem Solving

Directions: Use page 100 to answer these questions. First, skim the paragraphs to find information that might help you solve the problem. Remember to show your thinking as you do the math!

1. What shape is Nevaeh's closet? ____________

   When she drew a line to represent the shelf, into how many equal parts did she divide the closet? ____________

   What shape is each part? ____________

2. Nevaeh drew a picture of her closet on a piece of paper. She labeled the width 49 in. and the height 80 in.

   How many feet and inches wide is her closet? ____________

   How many feet and inches high is her closet? ____________

   Round the measurements to the nearest foot. ____________

   What is the area of her closet to the nearest foot? ____________

3. What shape is the space above the shelf? ____________

   How much of the area above the shelf would one stack of stuff represent? Write a fraction to show the amount of the whole. ____________

4. Nevaeh decided to put four bins below the shelf. Draw a picture to help you see how the bins would fit into the closet.

   How much of the bottom half of the closet would each bin take up? ____________

   What shape does each part represent? ____________

NAME ______________________ DATE __________

Engage **Directions:** Discuss with classmates how to divide space into parts with equal areas. Then, answer the questions below.

1. What is an area in the classroom that is divided into smaller areas? Draw and label a picture.

2. What shapes are the larger area and the smaller areas? ______________________

____

3. Write fractions to describe each part of the space. ______________________

____

4. Divide the space into three equal parts. What shape is each part? __________

How could one or more of the spaces be used? ______________________

____

Write a fraction to describe each part. ______________________

____

5. Think about a different way the space could be divided. Draw a new picture to show how the space would be used.

Answer Key

Smart Shopping (pages 7–9)

Problem Solving: 1. 30¢; 6 × 5¢ = 30¢ **2.** 30¢ × 6 = $1.80; the product **3.** 28 ÷ 4 = 7 items **4.** customer in checkout line A; (A) 48 ÷ 6 = 8 items per bag, and (B) 42 ÷ 7 = 6 items per bag; 8 > 6

Engage: 1. 7 bags × 5¢ = 35¢ saved; 7 bags × 10¢ = 70¢; 35¢ < 70¢; Shoppers save less money at Food Deals. **2.–3.** Answers will vary. **4.** 10 cents saved for each of the 7 cloth bags or the total amount saved with 7 cloth bags **5.** the number of cloth bags used if 35¢ was saved at a rate of 5¢ per bag

Cycling for a Medal (pages 10–12)

Problem Solving: 1. 30 teams; 150 riders ÷ 5 men on a team = *s* teams **2.** 45 teams; 180 riders ÷ 4 women on a team = *s* teams **3.** 6 hours; 25 miles per hour; Answers will vary. **4.** 150 miles ÷ 6 hours = *s* **5.** 215 minutes; 4 hours; 3 hours 35 minutes < 4 hours; She rode faster than 20 miles per hour.

Engage: Answers will vary.

Turf and Tree Farms (pages 13–15)

Problem Solving: 1. 2 ft. × 5 ft. = 10 sq. ft.; 10 × 8 = 80 sq. ft.; The roll can be drawn as a rectangle when it is unrolled; The unrolled sod can be tiled with one square unit tiles which shows that the width multiplied by the length is the total number of square units. **2.** 8 rows × (of) *a* rows each = 56 trees; *a* = 7 **3.** *b* rows × 10 trees each row = 107 trees; *b* = 10 rows, plus one more row with 7 trees **4.** 4 rows × (of) 30 trees = 120 trees; 120 trees + 1 row of 24 trees = 144 maple trees

Engage: 1. size of rolls, weight, how many will fit on the truck **2.** Some trees have been sold; Some trees did not make it through a cold winter or a summer heat wave. **3.** Answers will vary but may include thin or narrow trees (poplar, pillar oak, some cedar trees, others). **4.** 27 trees **5.** Answers will vary.

Eratosthenes: Prime Numbers (pages 16–18)

Problem Solving: 1. a number that can be divided exactly into a greater number **2.** Answers will vary. **3.** a number that has only 1 and itself as factors **4.** Write down the numbers between 1 and 100; Count by 2s and cross out all numbers that are multiples of 2.

Engage: 1. 1, 3, 9; no **2.** no; factors 1, 3, 5, 15 **3.–4.** Answers will vary.

Seven Times One (pages 19–21)

Problem Solving: 1. Seven times one are seven; 7 × 1 = 7; 1 × 7 = 7 **2.** It doesn't matter in which order two numbers are multiplied. **3.** Answers will vary but may include adding 1 set of a number to "six times" the number, thinking about square numbers, or thinking about the number of days in *n* weeks on the calendar. **4.** 1 × 1 = 1 **5.** The product is always equal to the number being multiplied by one.

Engage: 1. 7; The speaker says, "I am seven times one to-day." **2.** *Suggested answer:* the author's birthday **3.** Write a letter; Be trusted not to steal birds' eggs from nests. **4.** e.g., marybuds, columbine **5.** daisies, clover, lambs, moon, bee, marybuds (used to describe flowers of marigolds), columbine, purple flowers, bird's nest, linnet

The Ski Jump (pages 22–24)

Problem Solving: 1. 3 feet × $3 ski = $9; 6 arms × $4 pole = $24; 9 + 24 = $33; 2 arms × $4 pole = $8; 2 feet × $3 ski = $6; 8 + 6 = $14; $19 **2.** 4 feet × $3 ski = $12; $32 − 12 = *c*; *c* = $20, 20 ÷ $4 pole = 5 arms **3.** $66; $28 **4.** 74 rounded is 70; 15 rounded is 20; 70 × 20 = $1,400; $15 × 74 = (70 + 4) × 15 = (70 × 15) + (4 × 15) = 70 × 15 + 60 = 70 × (10 + 5) + 60 = (70 × 10) + (70 × 5) + 60 = 700 + 350 + 60 = $1,110

Engage: 1.–2. Answers will vary. **3.** Answers will vary; *Suggested answers:* safety; to make it possible to do the activity (e.g., skis for skiing) **4.** Answers will vary; *Suggested answers:* cost, time, being in shape, interest, weather **5.** Answers will vary.

Catch the Next Train (pages 25–27)

Problem Solving:

1.

	Yellow	Orange	Red	Green	Blue	Silver	Brown
Depart main terminal	12:00	12:00	12:00	12:00	12:00	12:00	12:00
Frequency	3 min.	4 min.	5 min.	7 min.	8 min.	9 min.	10 min.
Train 1	12:03	12:04	12:05	12:07	12:08	12:09	12:10
Train 2	12:06	12:08	12:10	12:14	12:16	12:18	12:20
Train 3	12:09	12:12	12:15	12:21	12:24	12:27	12:30
Train 4	12:12	12:16	12:20	12:28	12:32	12:36	12:40
Train 5	12:15	12:20	12:25	12:35	12:40	12:45	12:50
Train 6	12:18	12:24	12:30	12:42	12:48	12:54	1:00
Train 7	12:21	12:28	12:35	12:49	12:56	1:03	1:10
Train 8	12:24	12:32	12:40	12:56	1:04	1:12	1:20
Train 9	12:27	12:36	12:45	1:03	1:12	1:21	1:30
Train 10	12:30	12:40	12:50	1:10	1:20	1:30	1:40

2. 6 minutes; Every other time should be listed.
3. 1 minute; 2 minutes; 6 minutes **4.** 12:55

Engage: 1. Check colors for accuracy. **2.** The number of each train is also the number of minutes between each departure time. For example, there is one minute between each departure time for Train #1; there are two minutes between each departure time for Train #2. **3.–4.** Answers will vary.

Answer Key *(cont.)*

Modern Medicine Helps People (pages 28–30)

Problem Solving: 1. [current year rounded] – 1950 = *x*; [current year] – 1953 = *x* **2.** 9,000 – 2,300 = 6,700; 9,000 – 2,343 = 6,657 **3.** 27,000 – 9,000 = 18,000 cases; 27,000 – 6,000 = 21,000 people **4.** $\frac{35}{100}$

Engage: 1. Answers will vary. **2.** 4 doses; Answers will vary. **3.** 1953 – 1916 = 37 years **4.** 1947 – 1916 = 31 years **5.** 6,000 – 2,343 = 3,657; 2,343 + 3,657 = 6,000

Full of Life (pages 31–33)

Problem Solving: 1. 1776 + 83 = 1859; 1859 – 83 = 1776 **2.** 40 years old; 1859 – 40 = 1819 **3.** 100 years **4.** 1859 + 100 = 1959 **5.** 1959 + *n* = [current year]; Answers will vary; closer to two centuries **6.** Answers will vary: [current year] – 1859 = *n*

Engage: 1. He could be seen by people. **2.** The reader; The reader is reading the poem, and the poet is no longer alive. **3.–6.** Answers will vary.

Small Town U.S.A.: Walpi, Arizona (pages 34–36)

Problem Solving: 1. 7,185 – 1,124 = 6,061 people; 7,200 – 1,100 = 6,100; 6,100 + 1,100 = 7,200 **2.** 6,181 – 5,810 = 371 feet; 6,200 – 5,800 = 400 feet.; 5,800 + 400 = 6,200 feet **3.** 6,214 + 10 = 6,224 feet **4.** 900 years; [current year] – 900 = Answers will vary. **5.** [answer to question 4] + *a* = 1492; Answers will vary.

Engage: 1. Answers will vary but might include differences in plant life or climate. **2.** Answers will vary but might include living in a smaller or larger town. **3.** Answers will vary but might include 20 – 15 = 5 feet.

Charles Goodyear: The Rubber Man (pages 37–39)

Problem Solving: 1. 1844 – 1834 = 10 years **2.** 1839 + *x* = 1844; 5 years **3.** 1860 – 60 years = 1800; 1844 – 1800 = 44 years old **4.** 4 hours × 60 minutes = 240 minutes; 6 hours × 60 minutes = 360 minutes; 240 to 360 minutes **5.** 270 – 212 = 58 degrees **6.** 318,881,000 – 17,063,000 = 301,818,000 more people

Engage: 1. tires on cars and other vehicles; Answers will vary but might include carts, lawnmowers, and wheelbarrows. **2.** boots and raincoats; It is waterproof; Answers will vary. **3.** from trees; Answers will vary but might include tapping or draining a tree like syrup from a maple tree. **4.** Rubber wasn't stable; it melted in hot weather and became hard and cracked in cold weather. People weren't buying the products, and it wasn't useful. **5.** He added sulfur and lead and heated the mixture. **6.** plastic

Johannes Gutenberg: Books for Everyone (pages 40–42)

Problem Solving: 1. 70; 70 × 10 = 700 letter blocks **2.** 42 × 70 = (40 + 2) × 70 = (40 × 70) + (2 × 70) = 2,800 + 140 = 2,940 letter blocks **3.** 1,000 – 50 = 950 pages **4.** 200 copies ÷ 5 years = 40 copies per year

Engage: 1. About 30 lines of type; 30 × 70 letter blocks = 2,100 letter blocks **2.** Answers will vary; less than an hour **3.** 25 × 8 = 200 copies; 1 copy; Answers will vary.

A Land of Extremes (pages 43–45)

Problem Solving: 1. 2,000 × *a* = 6,000 feet; *a* = 3; 30 degrees drop; 112 – 30 = 82 degrees **2.** 2 inches; 2 inches × 30 = over 60 inches **3.** 1996 + 5 = 2001; 30 days × *a* months = 154 days; 30 × 5 = 150; *a* = 5 months **4.** 134 – 15 = 119 degrees **5.** 15 degrees × *b* = 75 degrees; *b* = 5 times warmer **6.** 32 degrees; 32 – 15 = 17 degrees; 32 + *b* = 134; *b* = 102 degrees; 212 degrees; 212 – 201 = 11

Engage: Answers will vary.

Picking Cotton (pages 46–48)

Problem Solving: 1. 4; 75¢; 3; $\frac{3}{4}$ **2.** 10; 50¢; 5; $\frac{5}{10}$ or $\frac{50}{100}$; $\frac{1}{2}$ **3.** 20; $\frac{5}{100}$ = $\frac{1}{20}$; $\frac{5}{20}$ **4.** 25¢; $\frac{1}{4}$ **5.** Yes, they are equivalent fractions; they represent the same amount or value of money; $\frac{5}{20} = \frac{1}{4}$

Engage: Answers will vary.

Our Earth: Water and Land (pages 49–51)

Problem Solving: 1. 5; $\frac{3}{4}$ **2.** Pacific Ocean; One-third of Earth should be shaded; Answers will vary. **3.** 7; They have different culture groups; Europe and Asia **4.** The Nile River is over 4,000 miles long; 400 ft. – 200 ft. = 200 feet shorter; the tides **5.** Number lines will vary.

Engage: 1. Answers will vary but might include large freshwater lakes (Great Lakes), deep canyons, or geysers. **2.** Missouri River (over 2,000 miles); It is about half the length of the Nile River. **3.** Mt. McKinley (Denali) is over 20,000 feet in elevation. **4.** Answers will vary but may include the vast amount of space on a continent. **5.** Answers will vary.

A New Bike Path (pages 52–54)

Problem Solving: 1. $\frac{1}{4}$, $\frac{1}{2}$, $\frac{3}{4}$, 1, $1\frac{1}{4}$, $1\frac{1}{2}$ **2.** 6 days **3.** 3 miles **4.** one inch; a line marked off at $\frac{1}{4}$, $\frac{1}{2}$, $\frac{3}{4}$, 1, $1\frac{1}{4}$, $1\frac{1}{2}$" on a number line that is $1\frac{1}{2}$" long or marked off at 3", 6", 9", 12" (one foot), 15" ($1\frac{1}{4}$ ft.), 18" ($1\frac{1}{2}$ ft.) [such a number line might be on another larger sheet of paper] **5.** $\frac{3}{4}$ mile

Engage: 1. Answers will vary. **2.** Answers will vary but might include quarter mile; 1 block **3.** Answers will vary. **4.** line segment $\frac{2}{3}$ of total distance **5.** Answers will vary.

Answer Key *(cont.)*

Pancakes Any Day (pages 55–57)

Problem Solving: 1. in halves, quarters, thirds, etc. **2.** one-third **3.** 9 thirds **4.** 8 fourths

Engage: 1. ingredients; amounts of ingredients; the order ingredients are added **2.** Answers will vary but should be reasonable. **3.** 2; 1; two **4.** 1956 recipe doubled:
$1\frac{1}{4}$ c. buttermilk + $1\frac{1}{4}$ c. buttermilk (number line diagram) = $2\frac{1}{2}$ c. buttermilk
2 T. oil + 2 T. oil = 4 T. oil
1 egg + 1 egg = 2 eggs
$1\frac{1}{4}$ c. flour + $1\frac{1}{4}$ c. flour (number line diagram) = $2\frac{1}{2}$ c. flour
1 teaspoon sugar + 1 teaspoon sugar = 2 teaspoons sugar
1 teaspoon baking powder + 1 teaspoon baking powder = 2 teaspoons baking powder
$\frac{1}{2}$ teaspoon baking soda + $\frac{1}{2}$ teaspoon baking soda = 1 teaspoon baking soda
$\frac{1}{2}$ teaspoon salt + $\frac{1}{2}$ teaspoon salt = 1 teaspoon salt

Concrete Everywhere (pages 58–60)

Problem Solving: 1. 14 pounds; $\frac{2}{14}$, $\frac{4}{14}$, $\frac{6}{14}$, $\frac{2}{14}$ **2.** 7 pounds; 1 pound; $\frac{1}{7}$; 2 pounds; $\frac{2}{7}$; 3 pounds; $\frac{3}{7}$; 1 pound; $\frac{1}{7}$

Engage: 1. It doesn't matter if you start with lime or clay first; It probably works best to add the water last. **2.** It doesn't matter which order you add the cement, sand, and rock; It probably works best to add the water last. **3.** addition and multiplication; subtraction and division **4.** *Suggested answer:* It doesn't matter if you put on your left sock or right sock first; It doesn't matter if you eat the sandwich or the fruit first in your lunch; You have to put socks on before shoes; It works better to toast the bread before you put butter on it. **5.** Answers will vary but may include buildings, bridges, or sidewalks.

A Five-Hundred-Year-Old Snack (pages 61–63)

Problem Solving: 1. $\frac{1}{2}$; Drawing should show a tortilla folded in half. **2.** like a triangle with one curved side **3.** 3 tortillas **4.** 4 people

Engage: 1. tortillas and cheese; In Spanish, it means "little cheesy thing;" It's a small snack that has cheese in it. **2.** native people in Mexico or Central America before the Spanish people came **3.** herbs, peppers, other vegetables, potatoes, chorizo, seafood, other types of meat **4.** Answers will vary but might include grilled cheese sandwich (cheese between two pieces of bread). **5.** Answers will vary.

Making Trail Mix (pages 64–66)

Problem Solving: 1. $1\frac{1}{2}$ cups almonds: 3 cups; $1\frac{1}{2}$ cups cashews: 3 cups; $\frac{3}{4}$ cup dried banana chips: $1\frac{1}{2}$ cups; 1 cup dried cranberries: 2 cups; $\frac{1}{3}$ cup dark chocolate chips: $\frac{2}{3}$ cup; $1\frac{1}{2}$ cups multi-grain cereal: 3 cups **2.** The recipe has equal amounts of almonds, cashews, and cereal. **3.** 3 times to make $1\frac{1}{2}$ cups; 6 times to make 3 cups **4.** 2 times to make $\frac{2}{3}$ cup **5.** more banana chips

Engage: 1.–2. Answers will vary. **3.** Graph should reflect that there are 7 cashews, 10 almonds, 4 dark chocolate chips, 9 dried cranberries, and 6 dried banana chips. **4.** The scale goes up to 10 because that's the highest number of ingredients.

A Red Moon (pages 67–69)

Problem Solving: 1. 120 minutes (2 hours) **2.** 209 minutes (3 hours 29 minutes); 5 minutes; 209 – 5 = 204 minutes; 3 hours 24 minutes **3.** 177 days; 26 + 31 + 30 + 31 + 31 + 28 = 177 days **4.** 76 minutes (60 + 16); 72 minutes (60 + 12); 2018; 4 minutes; a clock

Engage: 1. During a full moon, Earth and the sun and moon all line up; An eclipse happens when Earth's shadow covers the full moon. **2.** Earth's shadow completely covers the moon; Red light from the sun reflects best. **3.** A shadow covers the moon during a lunar eclipse; A shadow covers the sun during a solar eclipse. **4.–5.** Answers will vary.

Worth the Wait (pages 70–72)

Problem Solving: 1. 20 + 28 + 2 minutes = 50 minutes; 9:50 a.m.; 58 – 28 = 30 minutes **2.** Indiana Jones; 39 – 27 = 12 minutes; Big Thunder Mountain Railroad had a wait closest to half an hour. **3.** 30 (Big Thunder Mountain Railroad) + 40 (Indiana Jones) = 70 minutes; more than an hour; 27 + 39 = 66 minutes **4.** 1 hour 9 minutes **5.** 28 + 27 + 39 + 69 = 163 minutes; about 3 hours

Engage: Answers will vary.

Summer Eating Fun (pages 73–75)

Problem Solving: 1. 20 pounds × 500 g = 10,000 g **2.** 9 kg **3.** 3 kg **4.** 3,000 g + a = 10,000 g; 7,000 g more **5.** 268 – 20 = 248 pounds heavier; 134 – 9 = 125 kg more

Engage: 1. About $\frac{3}{4}$; 4 **2.** 15 pounds **3.** 3 cups × 20 pounds = 60 cups **4.** 60 **5.** 1 or 2 cups; If people eat more (watermelon is mostly water, it tastes good, people eat it in wedges instead of cups) than one serving, not as many people will be able to share one watermelon. Maybe closer to 20 people can share one watermelon.

Antoine Lavoisier: Chemistry for Everyone (pages 76–78)

Problem Solving: 1. 1 kg; 2 × 1,000 g = 2,000 g or 2 kg **2.** 6 parts out of 10 **3.** 200 mL **4.** 200 mL + 250 mL = 450 mL; 2,200 mL – 450 mL = 1,750 mL

Engage: Answers will vary.

Answer Key *(cont.)*

Recycling by the Numbers (pages 79–81)

Problem Solving: 1. *Suggested answer:* drawings of paper, plastic tub, plastic bags, glass bottle, cans; *suggested answer:* 5 or 10; paper, plastic, plastic bags, glass, aluminum (metal, tin cans) **2.** paper; plastics **3.** 55 − 27 = 28 **4.** 27 out of every 100; 27 × 10 = 270; 100 × 10 = 1,000; 1,000 − 270 = 730 items **5.** *Suggested answer:* Paper is visible and easy to recycle; Plastics can be confusing, or some places do not take all types of plastic.

Engage: 1. Number by 10s; 0, 100 **2.** *Suggested answer:* A bar graph might make it easier to understand information at a glance; They show the same information; A picture graph has pictures; A bar graph might show larger numbers and can be used for a wider variety of topics. **3.** Both categories of plastic are much lower than the other two categories; 27 pieces of glass + a = 63 pieces of paper; 36 more pieces of paper than glass recycled; 27 < 63 or 63 > 27 **4.** plastic and plastic bags; paper and plastic **5.** Answers will vary.

Croaks Around the World (pages 82–84)

Problem Solving: 1. 4; 4 **2.** $\frac{3}{4}$ and 1; $\frac{1}{4}$ inch **3.** $\frac{3}{4}$ inch + a = 2 inches; $a = 1\frac{1}{4}$ inches **4.** $1\frac{1}{2}$ inches − 1 inch = $\frac{1}{2}$ inch larger **5.** $1\frac{1}{2}$ inches + $b = 2\frac{3}{4}$ inches; $b = 1\frac{1}{4}$ inches

Engage: 1. line plot: $\frac{3}{4}$"—1 frog—small poison dart frog; 1"—1 frog—large poison dart frog; $1\frac{1}{4}$"—1 frog—male coqui frog; $1\frac{1}{2}$"—3 frogs—small red-eyed tree frog, African dwarf frog (male), female coqui frog; 2"—3 frogs—golden dart frog, African dwarf frog (female), American green tree frog; $2\frac{3}{4}$"—1 frog—large red-eyed tree frog **2.** 2 inches **5.** Answers will vary.

Shelter from a Storm (pages 85–87)

Problem Solving: 1. Answers will vary but length and width should be factors of 48. **2.** Perimeter will vary; 48 sq. ft. **3.** Answers will vary; Area should remain 48 sq. ft. **4.** 48 sq. ft. ÷ 4 people = 12 sq. ft. per person **5.** 4 people × 7 = 28 sq. ft.; 20 sq. ft. larger **6.** *Suggested answer:* Area describes the amount of space (square units) inside the shelter, which is where the people are. Perimeter describes the distance around the outside of a space, but that is not where people would go for shelter.

Engage: Answers will vary.

Let's Play Ball! (pages 88–90)

Problem Solving: 1. square or rhombus; four equal sides; opposite angles the same **2.** a square; It has 4 equal sides. **3.** pentagon; Answers will vary but may include helping the umpire see if a pitch is in the strike zone. **4.** circle **5.** rectangle; 4 sides; opposite sides the same length; 4 right angles

Engage: 1. inches **2.** square or rhombus; A rhombus has four equal sides and opposite angles are the same. A square has four equal sides and four right angles. The baseball field has four equal sides and four right angles. It is a square, or a special kind of rhombus. **3.** 90 in. **4.** Right angles: a square base bag fits in the corner.

Think Outside the Box (pages 91–93)

Problem Solving: 1. squares or rectangles that stack easily **2.** circles; cylinders **3.** Opposite sides are parallel; Opposite sides have equal lengths; It has four right-angle corners; The diagonal lines are the same size. **4.** Answers will vary but might include craft items or puzzles. **5.** All four sides are the same length; when the angles are not right angles

Engage: Answers will vary.

Wrapping a Gift (pages 94–96)

Problem Solving: 1. rectangular prism because it has height **2.** 6 **3.** a cube **4.** $\frac{1}{6}$ **5.** 10 × 4 = 40 sq. in.

Engage: 1. 160 sq. in.; 320 sq. in. **2.** 64 sq. in.; 128 sq. in. **3.** 80 sq. in. **4.** 42 sq. in.; no

Setting Up to Play (pages 97–99)

Problem Solving: 1. 16 ft. on each side; a square; from the name; All the sides are equal. **2.** 4 people; 4 **3.** They lay it down 5 times, then they need to move it one more time and mark 1 more foot. **4.** one-quarter, $\frac{1}{4}$; a square; 8 ft. × 8 ft. **5.** 16 ft. × 16 ft. = (10 + 6) × 16 = (10 × 16) + (6 × 16) = 160 + [6 × (10 + 6)] = 160 + (6 × 10) + (6 × 6) = 160 + 60 + 36 = 256 sq. ft.; 8 × 8 = 64 sq. ft.; Find the area of each person's playing space and add those areas together; 64 + 64 + 64 + 64 = 256 sq. ft.

Engage: 1. 16 + 16 + 16 + 16 = 64 ft.; 4 × 16 = 64 ft. **2.** length = 16 ft. edge + 6 ft. safety space on left + 6 ft. safety space on right = 28 ft.; width = 16 ft. edge + 6 ft. safety space on top + 6 ft. safety space on bottom = 28 ft.; area = 28 ft. × 28 ft. = 784 sq. ft. **3.** 6 ft. × 6 ft. **4.** 36 sq. ft.; 36 + 36 + 36 + 36 = 144 sq. ft.; no; Answers will vary.

Organizing a Closet (pages 100–102)

Problem Solving: 1. a rectangle; 2 equal parts; a rectangle **2.** 4 ft. 1 in.; 6 ft. 8 in.; 4 ft. wide, 7 ft. high; 4 × 7 = 28 sq. ft. **3.** a rectangle; $\frac{1}{3}$ **4.** $\frac{1}{4}$; a rectangle

Engage: Answers will vary.

Meeting Standards

Each unit meets one or more of the following Common Core State Standards () For more information about the Common Core State Standards, go to *http://www.corestandards.org/* or *http://www.teachercreated.com/standards/*.

MATH	
Operations & Algebraic Thinking	
Represent and solve problems involving multiplication and division.	**Unit**
CCSS.Math.Content.3.OA.A.1: Interpret products of whole numbers, e.g., interpret 5×7 as the total number of objects in 5 groups of 7 objects each. *For example, describe a context in which a total number of objects can be expressed as* 5×7.	Smart Shopping Turf and Tree Farms Eratosthenes: Prime Numbers The Ski Jump Catch the Next Train Summer Eating Fun Shelter from a Storm
CCSS.Math.Content.3.OA.A.2: Interpret whole-number quotients of whole numbers, e.g., interpret $56 \div 8$ as the number of objects in each share when 56 objects are partitioned equally into 8 shares, or as a number of shares when 56 objects are partitioned into equal shares of 8 objects each. *For example, describe a context in which a number of shares or a number of groups can be expressed as* $56 \div 8$.	Smart Shopping Cycling for a Medal Turf and Tree Farms Summer Eating Fun Shelter from a Storm
CCSS.Math.Content.3.OA.A.3: Use multiplication and division within 100 to solve word problems in situations involving equal groups, arrays, and measurement quantities, e.g., by using drawings and equations with a symbol for the unknown number to represent the problem.	Smart Shopping Cycling for a Medal Turf and Tree Farms Catch the Next Train A Land of Extremes Picking Cotton Worth the Wait Shelter from a Storm Setting Up to Play Organizing a Closet
CCSS.Math.Content.3.OA.A.4: Determine the unknown whole number in a multiplication or division equation relating three whole numbers. *For example, determine the unknown number that makes the equation true in each of the equations* $8 \times ? = 48$, $5 = \_ \div 3$, $6 \times 6 = ?$	Turf and Tree Farms The Ski Jump Summer Eating Fun Recycling by the Numbers Shelter from a Storm
Understand properties of multiplication and the relationship between multiplication and division.	**Unit**
CCSS.Math.Content.3.OA.B.5: Apply properties of operations as strategies to multiply and divide. *Examples: If* $6 \times 4 = 24$ *is known, then* $4 \times 6 = 24$ *is also known. (Commutative property of multiplication.)* $3 \times 5 \times 2$ *can be found by* $3 \times 5 = 15$, *then* $15 \times 2 = 30$, *or by* $5 \times 2 = 10$, *then* $3 \times 10 = 30$. *(Associative property of multiplication.) Knowing that* $8 \times 5 = 40$ *and* $8 \times 2 = 16$, *one can find* 8×7 *as* $8 \times (5 + 2) = (8 \times 5) + (8 \times 2) = 40 + 16 = 56$. *(Distributive property.)*	Turf and Tree Farms Seven Times One The Ski Jump Catch the Next Train Johannes Gutenberg: Books for Everyone Concrete Everywhere Summer Eating Fun Wrapping a Gift Setting Up to Play
CCSS.Math.Content.3.OA.B.6: Understand division as an unknown-factor problem. *For example, find* $32 \div 8$ *by finding the number that makes 32 when multiplied by 8.*	Cycling for a Medal Turf and Tree Farms Eratosthenes: Prime Numbers Antoine Lavoisier: Chemistry for Everyone Wrapping a Gift
Multiply and divide within 100.	**Unit**
CCSS.Math.Content.3.OA.C.7: Fluently multiply and divide within 100, using strategies such as the relationship between multiplication and division (e.g., knowing that $8 \times 5 = 40$, one knows $40 \div 5 = 8$) or properties of operations. By the end of Grade 3, know from memory all products of two one-digit numbers.	Turf and Tree Farms Eratosthenes: Prime Numbers Seven Times One The Ski Jump Catch the Next Train A Land of Extremes Picking Cotton Summer Eating Fun Shelter from a Storm
Solve problems involving the four operations, and identify and explain patterns in arithmetic.	**Unit**
CCSS.Math.Content.3.OA.D.8: Solve two-step word problems using the four operations. Represent these problems using equations with a letter standing for the unknown quantity. Assess the reasonableness of answers using mental computation and estimation strategies including rounding.	Cycling for a Medal Turf and Tree Farms The Ski Jump Small Town U.S.A.: Walpi, Arizona Charles Goodyear: The Rubber Man Johannes Gutenberg: Books for Everyone A Land of Extremes Picking Cotton Our Earth: Water and Land

Meeting Standards *(cont.)*

Operations & Algebraic Thinking *(cont.)*	
Solve problems involving the four operations, and identify and explain patterns in arithmetic. *(cont.)*	**Unit**
CCSS.Math.Content.3.OA.D.8: *(cont.)*	A Red Moon Summer Eating Fun Recycling by the Numbers Wrapping a Gift
CCSS.Math.Content.3.OA.D.9: Identify arithmetic patterns (including patterns in the addition table or multiplication table), and explain them using properties of operations. *For example, observe that 4 times a number is always even, and explain why 4 times a number can be decomposed into two equal addends.*	Seven Times One Catch the Next Train
Number & Operations in Base Ten	
Use place value understanding and properties of operations to perform multi-digit arithmetic.	**Unit**
CCSS.Math.Content.3.NBT.A.1: Use place value understanding to round whole numbers to the nearest 10 or 100.	The Ski Jump Modern Medicine Helps People Full of Life Small Town U.S.A.: Walpi, Arizona Charles Goodyear: The Rubber Man Johannes Gutenberg: Books for Everyone Worth the Wait
CCSS.Math.Content.3.NBT.A.2: Fluently add and subtract within 1,000 using strategies and algorithms based on place value, properties of operations, and/or the relationship between addition and subtraction.	Modern Medicine Helps People Full of Life Small Town U.S.A.: Walpi, Arizona Charles Goodyear: The Rubber Man Johannes Gutenberg: Books for Everyone Picking Cotton A Red Moon Antoine Lavoisier: Chemistry for Everyone Recycling by the Numbers
CCSS.Math.Content.3.NBT.A.3: Multiply one-digit whole numbers by multiples of 10 in the range 10–90 (e.g., 9×80, 5×60) using strategies based on place value and properties of operations.	Smart Shopping The Ski Jump Johannes Gutenberg: Books for Everyone A Land of Extremes Antoine Lavoisier: Chemistry for Everyone Recycling by the Numbers Wrapping a Gift
Numbers & Operations—Fractions	
Develop understanding of fractions as numbers.	**Unit**
CCSS.Math.Content.3.NF.A.1: Understand a fraction $\frac{1}{b}$ as the quantity formed by 1 part when a whole is partitioned into b equal parts; understand a fraction $\frac{a}{b}$ as the quantity formed by a parts of size $\frac{1}{b}$.	Picking Cotton Our Earth: Water and Land A New Bike Path Pancakes Any Day Concrete Everywhere A Five-Hundred-Year-Old Snack Making Trail Mix Summer Eating Fun Croaks Around the World Setting Up to Play Organizing a Closet
CCSS.Math.Content.3.NF.A.2: Understand a fraction as a number on the number line; represent fractions on a number line diagram.	Modern Medicine Helps People Our Earth: Water and Land A New Bike Path Pancakes Any Day Summer Eating Fun Antoine Lavoisier: Chemistry for Everyone Croaks Around the World
CCSS.Math.Content.3.NF.A.3: Explain equivalence of fractions in special cases, and compare fractions by reasoning about their size.	Picking Cotton Our Earth: Water and Land Pancakes Any Day Concrete Everywhere A Five-Hundred-Year-Old Snack Making Trail Mix

Meeting Standards *(cont.)*

Measurement & Data	
Solve problems involving measurement and estimation.	**Unit**
CCSS.Math.Content.3.MD.A.1: Tell and write time to the nearest minute and measure time intervals in minutes. Solve word problems involving addition and subtraction of time intervals in minutes, e.g., by representing the problem on a number line diagram.	Cycling for a Medal Catch the Next Train Charles Goodyear: The Rubber Man A Red Moon Worth the Wait
CCSS.Math.Content.3.MD.A.2: Measure and estimate liquid volumes and masses of objects using standard units of grams (g), kilograms (kg), and liters (l). Add, subtract, multiply, or divide to solve one-step word problems involving masses or volumes that are given in the same units, e.g., by using drawings (such as a beaker with a measurement scale) to represent the problem.	Summer Eating Fun Antoine Lavoisier: Chemistry for Everyone
Represent and interpret data.	**Unit**
CCSS.Math.Content.3.MD.B.3: Draw a scaled picture graph and a scaled bar graph to represent a data set with several categories. Solve one- and two-step "how many more" and "how many less" problems using information presented in scaled bar graphs. *For example, draw a bar graph in which each square in the bar graph might represent 5 pets.*	Making Trail Mix Recycling by the Numbers
CCSS.Math.Content.3.MD.B.4: Generate measurement data by measuring lengths using rulers marked with halves and fourths of an inch. Show the data by making a line plot, where the horizontal scale is marked off in appropriate units—whole numbers, halves, or quarters.	Croaks Around the World
Geometric measurement: understand concepts of area and relate area to multiplication and to addition.	**Unit**
CCSS.Math.Content.3.MD.C.5: Recognize area as an attribute of plane figures and understand concepts of area measurement.	Turf and Tree Farms Shelter from a Storm Wrapping a Gift Setting Up to Play Organizing a Closet
CCSS.Math.Content.3.MD.C.7: Relate area to the operations of multiplication and addition.	Shelter from a Storm Wrapping a Gift Setting Up to Play
Geometric measurement: recognize perimeter.	**Unit**
CCSS.Math.Content.3.MD.D.8: Solve real world and mathematical problems involving perimeters of polygons, including finding the perimeter given the side lengths, finding an unknown side length, and exhibiting rectangles with the same perimeter and different areas or with the same area and different perimeters.	Shelter from a Storm Let's Play Ball! Wrapping a Gift
Geometry	
Reason with shapes and their attributes.	**Unit**
CCSS.Math.Content.3.G.A.1: Understand that shapes in different categories (e.g., rhombuses, rectangles, and others) may share attributes (e.g., having four sides), and that the shared attributes can define a larger category (e.g., quadrilaterals). Recognize rhombuses, rectangles, and squares as examples of quadrilaterals, and draw examples of quadrilaterals that do not belong to any of these subcategories.	Let's Play Ball! Think Outside the Box Wrapping a Gift Setting Up to Play
CCSS.Math.Content.3.G.A.2: Partition shapes into parts with equal areas. Express the area of each part as a unit fraction of the whole. *For example, partition a shape into 4 parts with equal area, and describe the area of each part as $\frac{1}{4}$ of the area of the shape.*	A Five-Hundred-Year-Old Snack Wrapping a Gift Setting Up to Play Organizing a Closet

ENGLISH LANGUAGE ARTS	
Reading: Literature	
Key Ideas and Details	**Unit**
CCSS.ELA-Literacy.RL.3.1: Ask and answer such questions to demonstrate understanding of a text, referring explicitly to the text as the basis for the answers.	Seven Times One The Ski Jump Catch the Next Train Full of Life Picking Cotton Worth the Wait Setting Up to Play Organizing a Closet
CCSS.ELA-Literacy.RL.3.3: Describe characters in a story (e.g., their traits, motivations, or feelings) and explain how their actions contribute to the sequence of events.	Seven Times One The Ski Jump Full of Life A New Bike Path Making Trail Mix Wrapping a Gift

Meeting Standards *(cont.)*

Reading: Literature *(cont.)*	
Craft and Structure	**Unit**
CCSS.ELA-Literacy.RL.3.4: Determine the meaning of words and phrases as they are used in a text, distinguishing literal from nonliteral language.	Seven Times One Full of Life Picking Cotton A New Bike Path Making Trail Mix Worth the Wait Shelter from a Storm Setting Up to Play
CCSS.ELA-Literacy.RL.3.5: Refer to parts of stories, dramas, and poems when writing or speaking about a text, using terms such as *chapter, scene,* and *stanza*; describe how each successive part builds on earlier sections.	Seven Times One Full of Life
CCSS.ELA-Literacy.RL.3.6: Distinguish their own point of view from that of the narrator or those of the characters.	Full of Life Setting Up to Play Organizing a Closet
Integration of Knowledge and Ideas	**Unit**
CCSS.ELA-Literacy.RL.3.7: Explain how specific aspects of a text's illustrations contribute to what is conveyed by the words in a story (e.g., create mood, emphasize aspects of a character or setting).	Seven Times One Picking Cotton A New Bike Path
Range of Reading and Level of Text Complexity	**Unit**
CCSS.ELA-literacy.RL.3.10: By the end of the year, read and comprehend literature, including stories, dramas, and poetry, at the high end of the grades 2–3 text complexity band independently and proficiently.	*all*
Reading: Informational Text	
Key Ideas and Details	**Unit**
CCSS.ELA-Literacy.RI.3.1: Ask and answer questions to demonstrate understanding of a text, referring explicitly to the text as the basis for the answers.	Smart Shopping Cycling for a Medal Turf and Tree Farms Modern Medicine Helps People Small Town U.S.A.: Walpi, Arizona Charles Goodyear: The Rubber Man Johannes Gutenberg: Books for Everyone A Land of Extremes Our Earth: Water and Land Pancakes Any Day Concrete Everywhere A Five-Hundred-Year-Old Snack A Red Moon Summer Eating Fun Recycling by the Numbers Croaks Around the World Let's Play Ball!
CCSS.ELA-Literacy.RI.3.2: Determine the main idea of a text; recount the key details and explain how they support the main idea.	A Five-Hundred-Year-Old Snack A Red Moon Think Outside the Box
CCSS.ELA-Literacy.RI.3.3: Describe the relationships between a series of historical events, scientific ideas or concepts, or steps in technical procedures in a text, using language that pertains to time, sequence, and cause/effect.	Cycling for a Medal Eratosthenes: Prime Numbers Modern Medicine Helps People Small Town U.S.A.: Walpi, Arizona Charles Goodyear: The Rubber Man Johannes Gutenberg: Books for Everyone A Land of Extremes Pancakes Any Day Concrete Everywhere A Red Moon Antoine Lavoisier: Chemistry for Everyone Let's Play Ball! Think Outside the Box

Meeting Standards *(cont.)*

Reading: Informational Text *(cont.)*	
Craft and Structure	**Unit**
CCSS.ELA-Literacy.RI.3.4: Determine the meaning of general academic and domain-specific words and phrases in a text relevant to a *grade 3 topic or subject area.*	Smart Shopping Cycling for a Medal Turf and Tree Farms Eratosthenes: Prime Numbers Modern Medicine Helps People Charles Goodyear: The Rubber Man Johannes Gutenberg: Books for Everyone A Land of Extremes Our Earth: Water and Land Pancakes Any Day Concrete Everywhere A Five-Hundred-Year-Old Snack A Red Moon Summer Eating Fun Antoine Lavoisier: Chemistry for Everyone Recycling by the Numbers Croaks Around the World Let's Play Ball! Think Outside the Box
Integration of Knowledge and Ideas	**Unit**
CCSS.ELA-Literacy.RI.3.7: Use information gained from illustrations (e.g., maps, photographs) and the words in a text to demonstrate understanding of the text (e.g., where, when, why, and how key events occur).	Smart Shopping Small Town U.S.A.: Walpi, Arizona Johannes Gutenberg: Books for Everyone Our Earth: Water and Land Concrete Everywhere Making Trail Mix A Red Moon Recycling by the Numbers Croaks Around the World Let's Play Ball!
CCSS.ELA-Literacy.RI.3.8: Describe the logical connection between particular sentences and paragraphs in a text (e.g., comparison, cause/effect, first/second/third in a sequence).	Pancakes Any Day Croaks Around the World
Range of Reading and Level of Text Complexity	**Unit**
CCSS.ELA-Literacy.RI.3.10: By the end of the year, read and comprehend informational texts, including history/social studies, science, and technical texts, at the high end of the grades 2–3 text complexity band independently and proficiently.	*all*

Writing	
Text Types and Purposes	**Unit**
CCSS.ELA-Literacy.W.3.1: Write opinion pieces on topics or texts, supporting a point of view with reasons.	Turf and Tree Farms Full of Life Our Earth: Water and Land A Five-Hundred-Year-Old Snack Croaks Around the World Think Outside the Box Organizing a Closet
CCSS.ELA-Literacy.W.3.2: Write informative/explanatory texts to examine a topic and convey ideas and information clearly.	Charles Goodyear: The Rubber Man Pancakes Any Day Concrete Everywhere A Five-Hundred-Year-Old Snack A Red Moon Antoine Lavoisier: Chemistry for Everyone Setting Up to Play
CCSS.ELA-Literacy.W.3.3: Write narratives to develop real or imagined experiences or events using effective technique, descriptive details, and clear event sequences.	Turf and Tree Farms The Ski Jump Catch the Next Train Full of Life Small Town U.S.A.: Walpi, Arizona Antoine Lavoisier: Chemistry for Everyone Setting Up to Play

Meeting Standards *(cont.)*

Writing *(cont.)*	
Production and Distribution of Writing	**Unit**
CCSS.ELA-Literacy.W.3.4: With guidance and support from adults, produce writing in which the development and organization are appropriate to task and purpose.	Smart Shopping Cycling for a Medal Turf and Tree Farms Eratosthenes: Prime Numbers Seven Times One The Ski Jump Catch the Next Train Modern Medicine Helps People Full of Life Charles Goodyear: The Rubber Man Johannes Gutenberg: Books for Everyone A Land of Extremes Picking Cotton Our Earth: Water and Land A New Bike Path Pancakes Any Day Concrete Everywhere A Five-Hundred-Year-Old Snack Making Trail Mix A Red Moon Worth the Wait Summer Eating Fun Antoine Lavoisier: Chemistry for Everyone Recycling by the Numbers Croaks Around the World Shelter from a Storm Let's Play Ball! Think Outside the Box Wrapping a Gift Setting Up to Play Organizing a Closet
Research to Build and Present Knowledge	**Unit**
CCSS.ELA-Literacy.W.3.7: Conduct short research projects that build knowledge about a topic.	The Ski Jump Small Town U.S.A.: Walpi, Arizona A Land of Extremes Our Earth: Water and Land A Red Moon Antoine Lavoisier: Chemistry for Everyone Shelter from a Storm Think Outside the Box
CCSS.ELA-Litearcy.W.3.8: Recall information from experiences or gather information from print and digital sources; take brief notes on sources and sort evidence into provided categories.	Smart Shopping Cycling for a Medal The Ski Jump Catch the Next Train Small Town U.S.A.: Walpi, Arizona A Land of Extremes Our Earth: Water and Land Concrete Everywhere Making Trail Mix A Red Moon Worth the Wait Antoine Lavoisier: Chemistry for Everyone Recycling by the Numbers Croaks Around the World Shelter from a Storm Let's Play Ball!
Range of Writing	**Unit**
CCSS.ELA-Literacy.W.3.10: Write routinely over extended time frames (time for research, reflection, and revision) and shorter time frames (a single sitting or a day or two) for a range of discipline-specific tasks, purposes, and audiences.	*all*